# BEHAVIORAL MANAGED CARE

# BEHAVIORAL MANAGED CARE

## Strategies for Integrating Behavioral Health Services

M. J. Werthman, Ph.D.

**McGraw-Hill**

New York   San Francisco   Washington, DC   Aukland   Bogotá
Caracas   Lisbon   London   Madrid   Mexico City   Milan
Montreal   New Delhi   San Juan   Singapore
Sydney   Tokyo   Toronto

1 2 3 4 5 6 7 8 9 0 DOC/DOC 9 1 0 9 8 7

ISBN 0-7863-1092-8

This publication is designed to provide accurate and authoritative information in regard to the subject matter covered. It is sold with the understanding that neither the author nor the publisher is engaged in rendering legal, accounting, or other professional service. If legal advice or other expert assistance is required, the services of a competent professional person should be sought.

*From a Declaration of Principles jointly adopted by a committee of the American Bar Association and a Committee of Publishers.*

**Library of Congress Cataloging-in-Publication Data**

Werthman, M. J.
    Behavioral managed care : strategies for integrating behavioral health services / M. J. Werthman.
        p.    cm.
    Includes index.
    ISBN 0-7863-1092-8
    1. Managed mental health care—United States.    I. Title.
RA790.6.W47    1997
362.2'0425—dc21                                                96–51529
                                                                    CIP

*For Dr. Joan Barbara Doty, my mother and my friend*
*"Always remember your roots."*

# CONTENTS

# FOREWORD

Revolutionary changes are occurring in healthcare, particularly in mental health and substance abuse care. Rather quickly, almost 70 percent of the insured population in the United States is in some form of behavioral managed care. Despite stinging criticism, managed care has succeeded. Managed care in mental health and substance abuse has established a new framework for evaluating effectiveness. Effectiveness is now being judged on whether or not symptoms or behaviors that cause people to be nonfunctional are improved. Effectiveness is now being looked at scientifically and statistically to see if one delivery system is better than others. Effectiveness is now being looked at through sophisticated continuing quality-improvement techniques. Dr. Werthman explains this via writing about a hands-on understanding of how managed care works. She guides the readers to seeing the advantages to a comprehensive, clear understanding of what providers are expected to address and improve.

Managed care is redefining the mental health and substance abuse field. The reference for success is effectiveness and efficiency. Despite the criticism waged in the media, the main beneficiaries of this revolution are patients. Patients should benefit from new treatment techniques that will increase their rate of recovery. The cost of insurance has already been decreased by managed care. Dr. Werthman challenges preconceived views and enlightens her readers with how managed care increases effectiveness and efficiency.

**Bruce Roberts, M.D.**
**Regional Medical Director**
**Merit Behavioral Care**

# PREFACE

Currently, millions of people nationwide are enrolled in some form of behavioral managed care program, and billions of dollars are spent annually on the treatment of mental health and chemical dependency. According to the yearly survey conducted by Open Minds (May 1996), over 68 percent or approximately 124 million of those 181 million people who have health insurance are affected by behavioral managed healthcare. This percentage—which, by the way, reflects an almost 10 percent increase in the number of individuals enrolled in behavioral healthcare programs since last year's survey (March 1995)—attests to the significance of behavioral managed care as a rapidly growing industry. However, although this nation is actively participating in a behavioral healthcare revolution, much as it did a few years ago with medical healthcare, many consumers and providers (as well as payers, who themselves contract for behavioral managed care services) remain astoundingly in the dark about the goals, the operations, and the outcomes of this business. In addition, although behavioral managed healthcare evolved in response to and as a partial solution to the skyrocketing costs of more traditional indemnity and fee-for-service healthcare of prior years, behavioral managed care continues to incur significant criticism from the general public.

Change, no matter how beneficial in the long run, is often met with resistance. This response to change is frequently a result of fear, ignorance, and poor communication. Hence, given the relative scarcity of books on behavioral managed care, particularly from an insider's perspective, the public's need for accurate communication about the management of their mental health benefits and my own conviction that the process of behavioral managed care positively impacts patient care while containing costs for all parties, I was motivated to write this book. As a licensed psychologist currently employed as a case manager in a large behavioral MCO and as a provider of services myself within both public and private mental health organizations for over 15 years, I can empathize with the difficulties and challenges experienced by the

MCOs, the providers, and the consumers in this time of great change in behavioral healthcare.

Primarily, my intentions were twofold. First, I wanted to educate and convey necessary information to consumers, providers, payers, and other corporate entities about the process, thereby dispelling the fear, the ignorance, and the myths surrounding it. Second, in conveying practical clinical information, I hoped to ensure the probability of more positive and constructive relationships among consumers, providers, payers, and administrators to realize the common goal we shared—that of providing optimal patient care while containing healthcare costs for all. *Behavioral Managed Care: Strategies for Integrating Behavioral Health Services* is intended to enlighten the general public, whether that be the consumer, the CEO of a corporation, the payer, the health organization, the hospital, the group practice, or the individual provider.

This book is a how-to of managing mental health and chemical dependency treatment and provides practical insights, tips and information as well as a step-by-step approach to the industry from an insider's perspective. Readers will note that the terms *Behavioral MCO* or *Behavioral Managed Care Organization* are used throughout the course of this book. Although an MCO has typically been defined as representing a payer or an insurance company, its definition and usage in this book are somewhat different variables. A behavioral managed care organization (MCO) or a managed mental healthcare organization (MMHC) or a managed behavioral health program (MBHP) generally represent an entity or a system of financial, clinical, and administrative operations that controls or manages mental health and chemical dependency treatment within specified budgets for contracts that are either capitated or based on risk, performance, or some other standard.

These systems or entities can include specialty behavioral managed care firms, provider-managed service delivery systems, or government behavioral managed healthcare. This book utilizes the term *MCO* first in a broad sense as a system of clinical, financial, and administrative operations that applies the philosophy and principles of medical necessity guidelines to patient behavioral care. The term *behavioral MCO* is also utilized as it applies to specialty managed healthcare programs. In the latter usage, the behavioral managed healthcare part of an individual's benefit package is carved out (removed or separated) from the rest of that individual's benefit package. The payer, whether that be the employer, the union, or the insurance company, contracts with the company or the entity specializing in the management of mental health and chemical dependency treatment. The payer contracts with a behavioral MCO who will have the necessary clinical expertise, the ready service access, and often the available provider network to best manage their employees' or their enrollees' behavioral healthcare. These same companies may contract with another entity or MCO to manage the medical benefits of an individual's healthcare plan. Many of you are aware of several of the larger specialty behavioral MCOs such as Green Spring, Merit Behavioral Care, Value Behavioral Care, and Human Affairs International to name a few. Also, large employers and insurance companies may buy or develop their own specialty behavioral MCOs. Similarly, HMOs often contract through their own primary care physicians (PCPs) who manage referrals to mental health specialists.

After reading *Behavioral Managed Care*, the reader will have a practical working knowledge of:

1. The purposes and process of behavioral managed care.
2. The determination of a provider network.
3. The use of medical necessity criteria as it is applied to levels of care or to levels of treatment or containment.
4. The goals and limitations in the treatment of mental health and chemical dependency.
5. The significance of MCO–provider interactions.
6. The language of behavioral managed care.
7. Answers to commonly asked questions.
8. Claims issues.
9. Trends in the evolution of behavioral managed care.
10. Actual case scenarios and interchanges behind the scenes.

# ACKNOWLEDGEMENTS

With special thanks to my entire family and especially to the two Joans in my life, my mother and my daughter, for their inspiration and encouragement.

Appreciation also goes to my colleagues and friends at Merit Behavioral Care in Chicago, Illinois.

To my editor, Kris Rynne, for her help, and to my brother, George Werthman, also an editor, for his suggestions, I extend my thanks.

# BEHAVIORAL MANAGED CARE

# 1

# WHAT IS BEHAVIORAL MANAGED CARE, WHERE DID IT COME FROM, AND WHY DO WE NEED IT?

Behavioral managed care, a relatively recent phenomenon, has evolved within the context of medical managed care. The attempt to "manage" medical care originated as an attempt by large employers and insurance companies and later by the federal government to control skyrocketing healthcare costs while simultaneously providing services to as many people as possible given very limited financial resources. Although the concept of managing medical healthcare dates back almost 100 years, the actual deliberate and aggressive management of mental health and chemical dependency treatment as a financial and clinical venture began in the 1970s and early 1980s. Both corporate demands and heightened consumer awareness have played major roles in this behavioral healthcare revolution.

Corporate America, with its highly competitive and results-oriented focus, has increased its demands for high quality and increased productivity in the workplace. Further, corporate relocations, downsizings, expansions, and mergers have increased the need for flexibility and mobility on the part of workers. Longer, more intense work hours, the need for two incomes within families, and rapid technological advances have further stressed the American worker, resulting in an increase in mental health and chemical dependency problems. Employers are realizing the significant

1

negative impact of depression, anxiety, stress-related problems, poor morale, and substance abuse and dependence on employee work productivity and thus on the employer's ability to compete within the international and national arenas. The alarming increase in both work-related violence and work hours lost due to absenteeism has resulted in the expenditure of millions of dollars on medical costs by employers as well as by the government. Clearly, the epidemic of alcohol- and other substance-related disorders affecting individuals at home and in the workplace has raised concerns nationally. The increased incidence of drug use by adolescents and by children has also contributed to the rise in healthcare costs. Further, as lifespans have lengthened, the need for mental health and chemical dependency treatment has increased, thereby impacting national healthcare financing.

As national awareness of behavioral health problems has heightened, corresponding healthcare costs have spiraled upward. Employers and insurance companies, now more sensitive to the mental health needs of employees and their families and, at the same time, cognizant of rising costs, have begun to question the overall effectiveness of behavioral healthcare providers. Hence, the attempt to control costs while providing necessary treatment effectively has been a major impetus in the evolution of behavioral managed care as we know it today.

In summary, then, the rise of behavioral managed care has been propelled in large part by:

1. A heightened awareness nationally of the need for mental health and chemical dependency treatment in order to remain a competitive industrial nation.

2. A need to develop another type of behavioral healthcare financing and delivery system that is more efficient and less costly than traditional indemnity and fee-for-service systems.

3. A need to hold those providers of mental health and chemical dependency treatment accountable for observable, measurable, and visible outcomes.

Although these factors are by no means exhaustive, they have, in combination, significantly altered the course of behavioral healthcare delivery and financing. In the next chapter, the reader will review a description of the goals, parameters, evolution, and reasons for behavioral managed care in greater depth.

## DESCRIPTION OF BEHAVIORAL MANAGED CARE

Behavioral managed care, which is currently a multibillion dollar specialty industry affecting over 120 million people nationwide, carries with it several definitions. These definitions are rooted in both its historical evolution as well as its ultimate goals. Specifically, managed behavioral care is a specialty industry utilizing a set of integrated behavioral and financial systems that attempt to provide the highest quality patient care within the most appropriate and least restrictive treatment setting while ensuring cost containment. Behavioral managed care organizations (MCOs) are outgrowths of both HMOs (health maintenance organizations) and PPOs (preferred provider organizations) and, as such, utilize many of the structures, functions, and philosophies of these two health systems. Behavioral managed care has grown rapidly in response to the needs of HMOs and self-insured employer groups for more effective management of their substance abuse and mental health benefits. Behavioral MCOs contract with customers such as employers, unions, HMOs, and insurance companies to manage the mental health and substance abuse benefits for the customer's covered members. Although behavioral managed care models vary in terms of their financial structures, their management processes, and the particular means by which they deliver mental health and substance abuse services, they share much in common in terms of how they operationalize philosophies regarding high-quality patient care with concurrent cost control.

Regardless of the specific system, behavioral MCOs tend to share the following components, which are hallmarks of most MCO–customer business contracts with consumers (Shueman, Troy, and Mayhugh 1994):

1. Criteria for management and assessment of patient care.
2. Specific provider-behavioral managed care contracting.
3. Specific benefit structure.
4. Financial arrangement.
5. Behavioral managed care goals.

## Criteria for the Management and Assessment of Patient Care

In utilization review and case management, MCO clinicians apply specific treatment criteria or practice guidelines to forthcoming, existing, or ongoing types and levels of patient care to ensure appropriateness of care as well as cost containment. Behavioral MCOs subscribe to the philosophy that some individuals may require mental health and substance abuse treatment intermittently across their lifespans. They attempt to return a patient to his or her premorbid level of functioning as quickly as possible. MCOs attempt to eliminate unnecessary, inappropriate, and duplicate treatment services by carefully monitoring the type, the frequency, the intensity, and the duration of such services.

## Specific Provider-Behavioral Managed Care Contracting

The contracting between specific providers and behavioral managed care companies ensures a type of business agreement whereby providers perform specific treatment functions for which they are reimbursed by the managed care company. Specific providers may be individuals such as psychiatrists, psychologists, and social workers or facilities/institutions such as hospitals and VNAs (visiting nurses associations). This provider–MCO contracting attempts to foster mutual understanding and benefit to both parties. In essence, the provider agrees to provide mental health and substance abuse services at a discounted fee or a negotiated fee, depending upon the MCO-provider arrangement, in exchange for referrals from the MCO. The provider agrees to cooperate with the process of case management and utilization review applied by the MCO. The MCO is therefore able to manage care more directly and, ideally, will be able to provide quick and easy patient access to generalists and specialty providers within specific customer-dependent geographic locations. Frequently the customer or payer of behavioral MCO services will determine what types of providers will be utilized and what the necessary credentialing process for providers will entail.

## Specific Benefit Structure

This structure, defined largely by the customer or payer, describes covered and noncovered patient mental health and substance abuse services such that both providers and members or patients are encouraged to follow specific guidelines in their access to and utilization of benefits. Higher levels of care and more costly treatment methods, inpatient treatment for example, are discouraged except where medically necessary such as during crisis stabilization. Financial penalties may be exacted from both providers and patients for not precertifying with the MCO for admission to a higher level of care, thus shaping both patients and providers towards cost-effective utilization. Patients are generally encouraged to use in-network providers with whom the behavioral MCO has contracted for mental health and substance abuse services. Except where in-network service is not feasible geographically, the benefit for use of out-of-network providers is generally lower because the patient is required to pay a larger percentage, or co-pay. These factors enable the MCO to manage the mental health and substance abuse benefit, ensuring that medically necessary treatment criteria are met, while monitoring costs of treatment. However, it should be noted that immediate cost-containment is not always a factor in the MCO's decision to certify or not to certify treatment. Often MCOs will creatively utilize more costly treatment avenues such as VNAs, expert consults, and so on to maximize patient care and decrease recidivism, thereby reducing potential long-range costs.

Most customers/payers, in conjunction with behavioral MCOs, set forth a number of exclusions in mental health and substance abuse services that are generally not covered within the structure of the benefit. Commonly, these exclusions refer to the specific treatment of long-standing clinical illnesses where the treatment goals focus on the restructuring of personality such as in personality-disordered individuals. These exclusions may also apply to experimental treatments such as vitamin therapy and to treatments for the sole purpose of increasing self-discovery. These exclusions are understandable given the treatment philosophy of behavioral MCOs regarding brief, targeted treatment with the goal of returning an individual to a satisfactory, premorbid level of functioning as soon as possible. Hence, a behavioral MCO would generally certify treatment for a personality-disordered patient who is experiencing an acute psychotic illness; however, it is probable that the MCO would not certify treatment on the basis of an Axis II diagnosis alone as by definition, this diagnosis generally represents a stable and enduring disorder that persists into adulthood and is often treatment-resistant.

In some cases, the MCO may determine that it is necessary to certify a treatment that would ordinarily be considered an exclusion. This is known as *flexing* the benefit. Certification of excluded treatments is generally utilized when no other appropriate patient services are available and where certification of the particular patient treatment may achieve decreased recidivism and long-range cost reduction. A common example would involve certifying short-term residential treatment for an adolescent who is awaiting placement rather than simply discharging the patient from an acute inpatient setting.

## Financial Arrangement

This refers to the specific method by which the behavioral MCO receives monies from the customer who has purchased its services. There are various types of financial arrangements that exist between the MCO and the purchaser. Most commonly, purchasers of MCO services such as HMOs and employers contract with the MCO on a "capitation" basis whereby the behavioral MCO assumes financial risk for the administration of the purchaser's clinical benefits to its members. Generally, a capitation rate is the amount of money paid monthly to the MCO by the purchaser of the MCO's services and it "is based on the number of actual enrollees in (the purchaser's) plan that month" (Winegar 1992, 111). The capitation rate is a per member, per month monetary rate that is derived from the very careful evaluation by the MCO of the purchaser's member population regarding utilization of services, availability of provider services, the purchaser's proposed benefit structure including exclusions, as well as the particular MCO's track record regarding control over utilizations and costs. Once these variables are thoroughly researched, the MCO is able to propose a monthly rate per member, that will theoretically allow the MCO to provide and cover all the necessary clinical services to members, while covering the MCO's overhead as well as generating some degree of profit for the MCO. This capitation rate is multiplied by the purchaser's monthly membership to give the monthly capitation payment that the MCO will be paid by the purchaser (Winegar 1992). The importance of careful research in deriving a capitation rate cannot be overestimated, as failure to carefully assess utilization rates for a given membership as well as any loss of membership can have drastic effects on the MCO's ability to remain financially viable. Further, the type of management and the degree of clinical expertise within a given behavioral MCO will also determine subsequent profit or loss for the MCO.

This capitated arrangement enables the MCO, when successful, to realize profit and also gives the purchaser more direct control over the delivery of mental health and chemical dependency services. Other types of financial arrangements include a discounted fee for service, sliding scale fees, fee-per-admission, and fees based on a diagnosis-related group (DRG).

## Behavioral Managed Care Goals

Common in varying degrees to all MCOs are the following goals:

1. The provision of the highest quality of patient services at the most appropriate, least restrictive level of care in the most cost-effective manner.
2. The continued provision of mental health and chemical dependency treatment (Winegar and Bistline 1994) as well as the application of behavioral science principles in the treatment of problems that may affect both the physical and emotional well-being of a patient. These applications would include the treatment of chronic pain as well as the use of employee assistance programs to handle work performance problems.
3. The continued shaping and monitoring of individual providers as well as group providers (group practices, hospitals, etc.) regarding treatment and discharge planning such that providers themselves are held accountable for patient outcomes.
4. The easy and timely access by clients to a broad range of mental health and substance abuse treatments.
5. The ongoing effort to evaluate and objectify treatment outcomes as they relate to the patient, the provider, the behavioral MCO, and the client or payer company to determine the efficiency of current treatments as well as the direction of future treatments.

6. The careful screening, evaluation, and education of providers to ensure the highest quality patient services as well as the utilization of relatively uniform, scientific treatment approaches.

7. The ongoing scrutiny of existing community programs in the treatment of mental health and chemical dependency to more readily determine the medical necessity of such treatment approaches and to effect change in community services as appropriate.

8. The ongoing education of clinicians employed by MCOs in the use and application of medical necessity criteria to patient problems and to provider treatment goals and outcomes.

9. The commitment to patient and client satisfaction such that disputes arising from the certification or lack of certification of types and levels of patient care are managed through an orderly appeals and/or grievance process.

10. The commitment to a highly fluid and dynamic system of managing mental health and chemical dependency treatment such that individual patient needs can be met through a variety of treatment methods that can be questioned, modified, expanded on, and so forth.

## THE EVOLUTION OF BEHAVIORAL MANAGED CARE: WHERE DID IT COME FROM?

To understand the significance and use of behavioral managed care as an industry, it is critical to understand its long-range evolution as it relates to the growth of medical managed care as well as its short-range evolution as it relates to specific factors influencing the provision of mental health and substance abuse services. Although some researchers perceive the development of managed care, in general, as a result of the failure of previous healthcare systems (Sharfstein 1992), managed care can also be perceived as a dynamic and fluid system that has evolved and continues to evolve in response to the needs of patients, members, providers, purchasers, client companies, and national and local governments.

## Long-Range Overview

Behavioral managed care has its origins in the individual and government movement toward medical managed care. Over 100 years ago, those workers and their families who needed medical care paid for medical services out-of-pocket as if they were paying for any other service (Cafferky 1995). However, with the introduction of new, more efficient and advanced medical techniques, the cost of medical services as well as the demand for these services increased significantly (Baldor 1996). Prepaid medical groups, the beginnings of managed care, developed. Essentially, a prepaid medical group meant that for a monthly fee that was prepaid, or paid prior to services being rendered, physicians agreed to provide medical services for a defined population group. Blue Cross, the first health insurance plan (Baldor 1996) was developed from this concept of prepayment for medical services. This plan, which was the forerunner of other plans, initially paid for hospital admissions but did not cover outpatient visits or medication.

Managed care gained great impetus during the 1960s when the government developed the Medicaid and Medicare programs that helped finance health insurance for the poor, the elderly, and the disabled. However, the AMA (American Medical Association) resisted these government efforts because they were perceived both as a detraction from the autonomy and status of medical practice and as an attempt to socialize medicine. In response, the government compromised and gave hospitals and physicians the right to set their own prices for medical care, given the parameters of what was reasonable and customary. This began the era of price setting and fee-for-service models (Baldor 1996).

In 1973 the government passed the Health Maintenance Organization Act which forced specific employers to offer at least one federally funded HMO to their employees (Cafferky 1995) in addition to the traditional indemnity insurance plans. The development of the HMO was a direct government response to skyrocketing medical costs resulting from the fee-for-service plans and an attempt to provide responsible healthcare for lower income groups. An HMO, unlike the traditional indemnity plans, provides all medical care, including preventive care (e.g., immunizations and child care), for a negotiated flat fee that is paid up front as part of the annual insurance premium. It was during the development of HMOs that both Medicare and Medicaid staff attempted to manage more directly the medical care they were providing. Medicare is a federally funded insurance program covering the older population as well as the disabled, while Medicaid is the federally assisted and state-operated program providing health services to the poor and low-income groups. Traditional insurance plans as well as preferred provider organizations (PPOs) and the utilization review companies that were hired by PPOs began to copy the managed care techniques utilized by HMOs in reviewing and approving treatments (Cafferky 1995).

The HMO is often seen as the key impetus behind managed care as it is known today. The attempt to utilize management principles in directing and providing medical care fostered the growth of the current key elements in behavioral managed care, including case management, utilization review, various contracting models with providers, education of consumers, and the alternative use of community resources to provide various services (Cafferky 1995; Feldman and Fitzpatrick 1992), particularly during the 1980s and the 1990s. The increasing sophistication of managed care organizations in managing healthcare services has led to the concept of an integrated healthcare delivery system. Healthcare plan administrators as well as providers began to work together, contractually, toward the common goals of achieving high-quality patient care and patient satisfaction while maintaining cost control.

As of the writing of this book, the focus of behavioral managed care is on the empirical evaluation of treatment services to determine the quality and efficiency of treatment outcomes. Many individuals perceive the current and future realities of MCOs as encompassing managed outcomes (Waxman 1995). Although the treatment of behavioral healthcare problems is not as exact a science as the treatment of medical problems with subsequent, observable outcomes, such as hip replacement, bypass surgery, or even the control of common allergies through medication, behavioral healthcare can be translated into observable, measurable problems with achievable goals or outcomes. For example, if a patient presents with obsessive-compulsive disorder that results in frequent lateness to work, the treatment course may include medication and therapy to decrease the obsessive thoughts and ritualistic behaviors that interfere with the patient's arriving at work on time. One outcome measure would include, for example, the patient's timely arrival at work three out of five days due to the reduction in the frequency of disruptive thoughts and behaviors. This result would define the treatment rendered as a positive, measurable outcome. Similarly, if patient recidivism to acute inpatient hospitalization due to medication non-compliance because of adverse side effects is the defined patient problem, then treatment would include a medication reevaluation for effective medications that did not induce significant side effects. This adjustment would increase the probability of patient medication compliance and thus decrease recidivism. An outcome measure or indicator would include the frequency of rehospitalization within a given time span or length of time spent outside the hospital setting. Essentially, behavioral managed care is evolving to include not only definable problems and achievable goals but also measures of the success or failure of the treatment rendered.

## Precursors of Behavioral Managed Healthcare—
## Short-Range Overview

To better understand the current functioning of the industry of behavioral managed care, it is important to understand its roots. In particular, four basic precursors are noted: (1) community mental health centers (CMHCs), (2) health maintenance organizations (HMOs), (3) employee assistance programs (EAPs), and (4) telephone utilization review. (Freeman and Trabin 1994).

### Community Mental Health Centers (CMHCs)
Similarities between the philosophy of CMHCs and the philosophy of current behavioral MCOs are noteworthy. CMHCs arose as an attempt to deinstitutionalize patients from state hospitals by providing them with a continuum of less restrictive, community-based alternatives. The 1963 Community Health Centers Program was responsible for promoting communities as patient "catchment" areas and for providing mental health care to these patient populations. The concepts of easy accessibility, patient population, least restrictive setting, and continuity of care, which originated in CMHCs, are hallmarks in behavioral managed care today.

## Health Maintenance Organizations (HMOs)

The HMO Act of 1973 attempted to set minimal standards for the development of affordable healthcare for individuals from all socio-economic backgrounds. Because of the prepayment factor or the premium paid in advance of services, HMOs provided benefits for the treatment of mental health and substance abuse (MH/SA) greater than those provided by traditional indemnity plans in that they provided services which were preventative as well as restorative. Since HMOs assumed financial risk in the event that the cost of services was greater than the prepaid amount or premium, it was clinically and financially sound to offer a broader base of services which could help prevent illness and maintain health, thereby decreasing healthcare costs long-range. However, during the 1980s, traditional insurance plans increased their MH/SA benefit packages, while HMOs remained the same in terms of their benefits and were often inaccessible to patients due to limited provider groups in comparison to the large population served. Expanded services for MH/SA began to develop as a result of "carve-out" behavioral managed care companies, which served employers and other clients or purchasers. Today many HMOs have created their own behavioral managed care carve-outs, while others have purchased the services of specialized behavioral MCO vendors to manage their mental health and substance abuse benefits.

## Employee Assistance Programs (EAPs)

Employee assistance programs (EAPs), which evolved in the 1950s, targeted early intervention for alcohol and drug abuse (Freeman and Trabin 1994) and gradually expanded their services to employers and employees. EAPs were significant in their abilities to gain access to appropriate treatment for patients within a very large and complex healthcare system. Currently behavioral managed care utilizes many of the strong points of EAPs including their ability to develop triage criteria and to triage patients to the appropriate level of care and their formation of a trusted network of providers (Freeman and Trabin 1994).

## Utilization Review (UR)

Utilization review by telephone, which originated in the 1970s and escalated in the 1980s, began primarily with a focus on medical-surgical cases. These UR companies altered their procedures to further include the utilization review of mental health and substance abuse cases. UR companies, which focused on inpatient preadmission and concurrent reviews, were instrumental in making certification or authorization a requirement for financial reimbursement, even though UR companies did not, at that time, have established contracts with providers such as hospitals (Freeman and Trabin 1994).

However, because early UR companies focused on review of medical-surgical cases, with RNs reviewing under the supervision of physicians, these companies were not fully equipped to review the more specialized, less concrete areas of behavioral mental health and chemical dependency. As a result, many UR companies either purchased the services of a specialized behavioral care company to do utilization review or else formed their own.

Another significant factor in the growth of UR companies was the contractual agreement between CHAMPUS (the Civilian Health and Medical Program of the Uniformed Services) and the two APAs (American Psychiatric Association; American Psychological Association) to develop criteria for retrospective peer review in the 1970s.

UR companies were successful in reducing inpatient admissions and utilization; however, outpatient services increased significantly. Also, UR companies, which lacked contractual relationships with providers (i.e., hospitals, facilities, etc.), often developed hostile and adversarial relationships with providers such that they were no longer able to monitor cost and quality of care. Further, impetus for the development of carve-out behavioral managed care companies resulted from these problems.

By the 1980s, healthcare costs were skyrocketing, and quality of care was no longer a driving factor as little information was available about providers and treatment outcomes. At the same time, private, for-profit organizations utilized the media to promote their services and facilities, thereby reducing the stigma associated with psychiatric problems and chemical dependency problems and increasing the demand for help in overcoming them. It was during this time period that the 28-day inpatient chemical dependency program became standard, as did lengthy inpatient hospitalizations for troubled adolescents and long-term self-discovery outpatient therapies (Freeman and Trabin 1994). The loss of control over both healthcare costs and quality set the stage for behavioral managed care to become a specialty industry.

Behavioral managed care companies have frequently developed from small provider groups who offered services to businesses within a given geographic location, from UR companies who have contracted with networks to provide a continuum of services, and from EAPs that have expanded into the behavioral managed healthcare arena.

The growth and development of behavioral MCOs has been unpredictable at times and has followed unchartered waters, thus reinforcing its need for dynamism, fluidity, and flexibility. From the period of the 1980s with its high-gear marketing to employers and to insurance companies, for example, to the early 1990s, a period of buyouts, mergers, and acquisitions by managed care companies as well as by employers and insurance companies, the industry of behavioral managed care has undergone a period of consolidation.

## THE EVALUATION OF BEHAVIORAL MANAGED CARE: THE PROS AND CONS

Behavioral managed care, or managed mental health and substance abuse care, is a relatively new and evolving system. Although the treatment of mental health problems and chemical dependency has long been practiced in one form or another, the endeavors by MCOs to administratively and clinically manage treatment through the application of more scientific and observable criteria is new. It is not surprising, then, that behavioral managed care has been received with a certain degree of skepticism and criticism. The significance of and the need for the behavioral managed care industry is best determined by reviewing the types of criticisms leveled against it.

The 10 most common criticisms of behavioral managed care, as well as counterarguments in favor of behavioral managed care are discussed in the following sections.

### The Issue of Patient-Therapist Confidentiality

Although traditional third-party payers have always requested some type of clinical information, whether it was a diagnosis or a description of services, the advent of behavioral managed care has brought with it significantly increased expectations for clinical documentation. Further, managed care case managers and reviewers are in ongoing communication with participating providers about individual patients' problems and treatment plans, weighing treatment episodes of care against medical necessity criteria. For these reasons, many critics have questioned the degree to which behavioral MCOs are able to maintain patient-therapist confidentiality (Kelly 1994; Shueman, Troy, and Mayhugh 1994).

### Con A
Those opposed to managed care have cited various potential and actual problems inherent in their ability to maintain confidentiality of patient disclosure. Given the current information systems available, many fear that such large amounts of sensitive data can be accessed all too readily by any number of people. Providers and consumers fear that managed care companies cannot guarantee safety regarding the responsible use of such sensitive patient information.

### Pro A
Managed care companies, however, have asserted that they enforce strict policies regarding confidentiality, utilizing hard copy clinical data and when utilizing information systems, using passwords and other means for ensuring only appropriate access. Further, they have argued that only the patient (or guardian) can sign a release of information such that clinical information would be disclosed to third parties such as employers.

### Con B
Another criticism regarding confidentiality is the concern expressed by patients and providers alike that the questioning of and data gathering from providers done by managed care reviewers and case managers will destroy any sense the patient may have regarding privacy. Providers argue that in certain cases this intrusiveness can negatively affect the treatment process and its outcomes (Kelley 1994).

### Pro B
Behavioral managed care companies assert that the information gathered by their reviewers includes only that information necessary to reach a responsible decision about quality of care and medical necessity of treatment. In-depth analysis of patient problems and background is not generally the job description of a reviewer or a case manager. According to MCOs, a breach of confidentiality by a staff member would result in the termination of that particular individual.

## The Issue of Patient–Therapist Bonding (Therapeutic Alliance)

The hallmark of therapy, according to many, is the ability of the patient to form a therapeutic alliance, or bond, with the therapist (Sharfstein 1992). This bonding is the basis for the therapeutic process between patient and therapist.

### Con A

Opponents of behavioral managed care have argued that third-party oversight and involvement in the therapeutic process negatively impacts the bonding process. Further, opponents argue that this third party, the managed care reviewer or case manager, through his or her intrusiveness, threatens the trust-building in therapy and places the provider in a defensive position. The use of third-party oversight casts doubt on the ability, judgment, and skills of the provider, further challenging the bonding relationship. Providers have also argued that MCO staff often appear to lack the appropriate level of training for the process of reviewing with a mental health professional (Kelley 1994).

### Pro A

Managed care companies, who themselves employ clinicians, do agree that the processes of utilization review and case management have some type of effect on the bonding process; however, the type and extent of such an impact is not yet known (Shueman, Troy, and Mayhugh 1994). They further argue that providers are finally being held accountable for their performances. This heightened accountability may serve to weed out less proficient clinicians and make the process of therapy more effective and targeted for the patient. MCOs also note that although some patients and some providers view the third-party oversight as negatively impacting the patient–therapist relationship, overall the benefits of utilization review and case management may outweigh the negatives. Empirical research on this subject is still in its infancy, however, and outcome studies are just currently underway.

## The Issue of Treatment Restrictions

The guiding principles of behavioral managed care include the provision of high quality, medically necessary treatment in the least restrictive environment, while containing costs.

**Con A**

Critics of managed care have argued that these basic MCO tenets discriminate against certain types of patients with regard to treatment access and frequency, intensity, and quality of treatment. Specifically, the personality-disordered patients and the more chronic or severely disabled patients are perceived by many providers as short-changed when it comes to treatment options. Routinely, providers have argued that managed care gives up on some patients (Kelley 1994) and will not cover needed services for others.

**Pro A**

Proponents of managed care argue that all patients have access to focused and targeted treatment throughout their lifespans. This includes the types of patients (e.g., personality-disordered, chronically mentally ill) whose diagnoses by definition indicate chronic conditions, but who have, at various points, the need for stabilization, intervention, and support. Further, many MCOs are becoming increasingly sophisticated about employing nontraditional, innovative clinical options for these often high-recidivist and chronic patients. For example, it is routine in some MCOs to offer expert consults, VNA, and home healthcare services as well as intensive medical management and psychotherapy for patients who would typically have been contained within an inpatient environment, or a custodial care setting.

Although, like many providers, MCOs do not expect to cure specific chronic illnesses, they assert that appropriate and medically necessary treatment is readily accessible to return individuals to an acceptable level of functioning that enables them, for the most part, to operate within their immediate environments.

## The Issue of Denial of Care

Along with the application of medical necessity criteria, many behavioral MCOs are moving toward assuming greater financial risk in their management of mental health and substance abuse benefit plans for employers. Behavioral managed care is evidencing much growth as a business and as an industry, and greater financial risks generally result in greater control over the administration of benefits, clinically and administratively. It also may well result in larger profits for managed care companies.

### Con A

Opponents of behavioral managed care argue that such a financially driven business approach undermines sound clinical expertise and treatment by motivating MCOs and individual MCO staff to find treatment medically unnecessary or to deny access to care inappropriately. Compounding this problem has been the fact that until recently MCOs utilized medical necessity practice guidelines or criteria that were unknown to providers except by trial-and-error learning.

### Pro A

Today MCOs have become highly sensitized to the issue of denial of care for monetary gain. They argue that employers and other purchasers of their services are more attuned to the particular needs of their member populations and, hence, are more astute and more demanding of appropriate, high-quality clinical services. Further, many MCOs currently make a point of hiring individuals with solid clinical credentials as contract managers for contracts they are servicing. According to MCOs, this shift enables the contract manager, who is the liaison between the MCO and the purchaser of member services, to ensure appropriateness and quality of treatment for recipients of care. In collaboration with purchasers, MCOs also have instituted various levels of appeal for providers as well as for members when access to care is denied. MCOs have responded to criticism from providers who claim they are being judged against unknown criteria by publishing their criteria or practice guidelines.

## The Issue of MCO Staff and Quality of Performance

Behavioral managed care companies routinely provide case management and utilization review to determine the medical necessity of treatment as well as the appropriateness of treatment planning, and so on. The roles of case manager and utilization reviewer have been filled by staff drawn from a variety of backgrounds.

### Con A

Opponents of behavioral managed care have argued that case managers and utilization reviewers are not up to the task of managing quality of care. They argue that staff are poorly trained, lack clinical expertise and competence, and are unfamiliar with the care to which they are applying medical necessity criteria. Furthermore, these opponents increasingly argue that case managers and reviewers are difficult to reach by phone and demand too much time from providers whose schedules are already overbooked.

**Pro A**

Behavioral managed care companies have argued that they, like other industries, are evolving. As such, they have become more selective in the qualifications of staff they hire. Currently, many of the larger MCOs employ clinical case managers and reviewers who are licensed to practice independently. MCOs have reported that they are hiring more qualified and experienced individuals including social workers and psychologists. Additionally, many behavioral MCOs have instituted various types of internal, ongoing training for their employees in state of the art diagnostic and treatment approaches.

## The Issue Regarding the Role of the PCP (Primary Care Physician)

With the advent of significant healthcare reforms, the increasing demand for greater impact by primary care physicians (e.g., PCPs, family practitioners, internists) has been noteworthy. The role of the PCP as gatekeeper in the specialist-referral process has, in part, expanded the role of the PCP to performing such functions as providing mental healthcare to patients in lieu of making a referral to a specialist provider.

**Con A**

Opponents of behavioral managed care blame MCOs for dumping responsibility on PCPs inappropriately due to healthcare restrictions that limit patients' access to specialists in mental health, the types of treatment they may receive, as well as the number of sessions they may utilize. Opponents further argue that PCPs generally lack clinical expertise in the field of mental health and substance abuse and, thus, sacrifice quality of care by underreferring and underdiagnosing (Kelley 1994).

**Pro A**

MCOs have counterargued that the shift in the role of the PCP simply reflects greater integration of mental health and substance abuse services. They further argue that most PCPs do refer patients to mental health and substance abuse specialists when conditions so indicate.

### The Issue of Patient/Consumer Knowledge

While billions of dollars are spent yearly on the treatment of mental illnesses and chemical dependency, approximately 124 million people nationwide are impacted by some type of behavioral managed care plan, and over 25 percent of the total healthcare budget is spent on the costs of treatment for mental health and substance abuse problems, most consumers remain unenlightened about behavioral managed healthcare.

### Con A
Opponents of behavioral managed care argue that the consumers (patients, members, etc.) are frequently mislead by MCOs. These opponents argue that although MCOs purport to manage clinical care, they really are managing the benefit such that patient problems are structured within the confines of the benefit. Further, these opponents report that consumers are often mislead into believing they have unlimited benefits when in fact, the MCO may only allot three days of inpatient care and five outpatient sessions, for example.

### Pro A
Behavioral managed care companies counter these arguments with the concept that medically necessary treatment is not necessarily the same as medically desirable. In other words, a particular patient may not access every type of treatment that he or she wants but only what is medically necessary, given the problem at hand. Further, MCOs argue that more is not necessarily better in terms of treatment frequency, intensity, and duration.

## WHY DO WE NEED BEHAVIORAL MANAGED CARE?

Behavioral managed care is an evolving, fluid system that is still in its infancy. As such, it will continue to draw fire from critics and particularly from providers who perceive this specialty industry as a deliberate assault on their professional autonomy as well as on their financial independence. However, the behavioral managed care industry's demand for provider accountability is long overdue, according to many proponents. The industry, which has attempted to correct the shortcomings of previous provider healthcare systems, is, in part, an advocate for the patient or member. By demanding that specific standards of patient care be met and by questioning and / or denying what it perceives as unnecessary or duplicate services, it fosters higher quality of care as well as cost savings for both the member and the client or customer. As behavioral MCOs become more sophisticated, the demand for alternative community services as well as the demand for increased provider expertise will also increase.

The following factors, which will be expanded on later, have contributed to the success of current behavioral MCOs. These factors speak to the why of behavioral managed care.

***Quick, Easy Accessibility of Services***   A primary focus of current MCOs is the attempt to afford patients quick, easy access to providers in a broad range of geographic areas. Most MCOs even make provisions for patients to see providers who are Nonnetwork or who are not participating in the MCO's network.

***Reduced Costs***   Most behavioral MCOs are engaged in contracts with purchasers in which they financially share healthcare risk. As such, MCOs aggressively attempt to provide the highest level of patient care by targeting appropriate treatment and by eliminating medically unnecessary and duplicate services.

***Quality Assurance Mechanisms***   MCOs are invested in their processes as well as in treatment outcomes. They are reviewed by accrediting bodies for compliance with quality standards. As such, MCOs monitor for appropriate treatment and discharge planning of patients. MCOs are currently focusing on methods for the evaluation of treatment outcomes.

***High Patient Satisfaction***   MCOs continually survey patients as to their degree of satisfaction with treatment. Problems and criticisms are addressed by customer service and provider relations departments.

***Coordination of Care***   One of the hallmarks of behavioral MCOs is their ability to ensure continuity of care through their trained staff. In other more traditional health plans, patients are generally left on their own to do this. MCOs pride themselves on their ability to enable patients to access various types of care and to ensure that patients are appropriately transitioned to lower levels of care, where appropriate.

***Case Management and Utilization Review***   These functions, also hallmarks of behavioral MCOs, ensure provider accountability when it comes to patient care. These functions serve to ensure that patients are receiving appropriate treatment and that staff employed in these functions intervene in cases where patient care is inappropriate or below standard. These functions are vital to the survival of MCOs.

***Medical Necessity of Care and the Appeals Process*** When disagreements in care provided arise, the patient or member, as well as the provider, have recourse to challenge an MCO's decision. This review of the medical necessity of care generally is handled through an appeals process in which various levels of review with outside providers take place.

***Availability of Alternative Services*** Unlike traditional healthcare, MCOs pride themselves on their ability to provide alternative services to their patients in need, such as expert consults, VNA, and other specialized treatment. MCOs often access the least intrusive care methods, which are not always readily available in the community. At times, an MCO may even flex a benefit, or provide a level of care, such as residential treatment which may not be a covered benefit, in the interest of increased patient quality of care and decreased recidivism.

***Provider Education and Profiling*** This function ensures that patients are afforded the best care necessitated by the specific treatment episodes. Providers are continually monitored for quality and treatment outcomes, and complaints about particular providers are handled by MCOs internally. Also, providers are trained in state of the art methods for treating particular problems.

***Prevention and Intervention*** By using medical necessity criteria and by following individual patient cases for continuity and quality of care, MCOs are able to intervene in treatment episodes and to provide follow-up care to prevent or curtail future treatment episodes. By asking questions about the precipitant of particular treatment episodes, MCOs are often able to offer suggestions regarding prevention and intervention.

To meet the primary goals of behavioral managed care, that of providing optimal patient treatment in the least restrictive environment while containing costs, the behavioral MCO must have some degree of administrative, clinical, and financial control over the treatment delivery system. The next chapter provides an overview of key components in the behavioral MCO operation: network development and provider management. These two components can often make or break a developing MCO.

## REFERENCES

Baldor, Robert A. 1996. *Managed Care Made Simple.* Cambridge, MA: Blackwell Science, Inc.

Cafferky, Michael E. 1995. *Managed Care and You: The Consumer's Guide to Managing Your Health Care.* New York: McGraw-Hill.

Feldman, Judith L., and Richard Fitzpatrick, eds. 1992. *Managed Mental Health Care: Administrative and Clinical Issues.* Washington, DC: American Psychiatric Press, Inc.

Freeman, Michael A., and Tom Trabin. 1994. *Managed Behavioral Health Care: History, Models, Key Issues, and Future Course.* Rockville, MD: Paper prepared for the U.S. Center for Mental Health Services, Department of Health and Human Services, October .

Kelley, Timothy. 1994. 10 Charges Leveled against Managed Mental Health Care. *Managed Care: A Guide for Physicians* 3, no. 10 (October): 22–26.

Sharfstein, S. S. 1992. Managed Mental Health Care. In *Review of Psychiatry* 11, ed. A. Tasman and A. B. Riba, 570–84. Washington, DC: American Psychiatric Press.

Schueman, Sharon A., Warwick G. Troy, and Samuel L. Mayhugh, eds. 1994. *Managed Behavioral Health Care: An Industry Perspective.* Springfield, IL: Charles C. Thomas Publishing.

Winegar, Norman. 1992. *The Clinician's Guide to Managed Mental Health Care.* New York: The Haworth Press, Inc.

Winegar, Norman, and J. L. Bistline. 1994. *Marketing Mental Health Services in a Managed Care Environment.* New York: The Haworth Press, Inc.

# CHAPTER

# 2

# PROVIDER SELECTION AND CONSUMER CHOICE

The development and maintenance of a provider network are essential components of most behavioral managed care companies. It is important to understand the rationale involved in the development and ongoing maintenance of such arrangements, given the MCOs' goal of providing high-quality patient care that is also cost-effective. The network includes individual providers such as psychiatrists, psychologists, social workers, alcohol and drug counselors, family practitioners, clinical nurses, and so on and larger, organized systems of providers, including hospitals with their inpatient, partial hospitalization and intensive outpatient programs, as well as alcohol and drug programs, residential settings, and community outpatient settings. Generally, these providers have agreed to provide services to members and their families who are covered by specific MCO-purchaser contracts in return for a prearranged set of reimbursements depending on the service model utilized. Further, these providers generally have agreed to engage in the utilization and case management processes and also have agreed to follow the particular MCO's set of guidelines regarding medically necessary treatment, continuity of treatment, and termination of treatment. In short, these providers have agreed to the various standards of performance and accountability set by the particular behavioral managed care company with whom they have contracted.

The rationale for developing a provider network is to increase the MCO's clinical control over the particular system or contract that they are servicing by ensuring greater accountability and greater consistency in quality of care provided. Additionally, MCOs have greater financial control over service costs by negotiating and setting generally discounted fee-for-service reimbursement schedules for providers in exchange for their services. Behavioral MCOs attempt to ensure quality and easy accessibility of care for contract members by maintaining a network of providers in a specified geographic location. Having a prescreened network of providers from which to choose decreases the likelihood of choosing providers who are inappropriate. MCOs are also able to offer a continuum of care by contracting with group providers such as hospitals where patients can be readily "stepped down" to increasingly less restrictive treatments within the same setting of the hospital if appropriate. Further, case managers and utilization reviewers are better able to monitor treatment outcomes and quality by utilizing a provider network with which they have become familiar.

## DETERMINANTS OF A PROVIDER NETWORK

The success of a particular provider network is largely dependent on its satisfaction of characteristics related to size, location, and composition (Shueman, Troy and Mayhugh 1994).

### Network Size

It has often been thought that having a very large network ensures availability and quality of services; however, this is not necessarily true. For most MCOs, the key to successful provider networks is to have a network of providers large enough to meet various treatment needs but not so large that MCO staff (i.e., case managers, utilization reviewers) cannot familiarize themselves with providers' particular strengths and competencies. Theoretically, the provider networks should be fitted to the specific client and membership it is servicing. The fit ideally should be made after the MCO has familiarized itself with the utilization rates, characteristics, and problems commonly associated with a particular membership or member group. A membership group consisting of electricians and their families may have a different set of utilization rates than a beneficiary group consisting of bank personnel. For example, electricians as a group may have a higher frequency of treatment needs related to periods of unemployment that require a different type of treatment utilization than bank personnel, who as a group may have a higher frequency of treatment needs related to theft.

The size of a provider network also influences the number and frequency of referrals to particular providers with smaller networks generating a greater number of referrals to specific providers. Often, the greater the number of referrals to a particular provider or provider group, the more positively the MCO-provider relationship develops. However, this is not always the case, particularly in those instances where MCOs are forced to choose providers by default because of a scarcity of resources in a particular geographic area.

Ideally behavioral MCOs have spent time, resources, and careful planning in establishing a provider network. However, often this is not the case. Due to the highly competitive nature of the behavioral managed care industry, behavioral MCOs often find themselves pulling networks together at the last minute to accommodate new or changing customer contracts.

## Geographic Area

Commonly, MCOs must ensure that their networks cover a wide enough geographic area to allow access to a variety of services by the particular members or beneficiary group they are servicing. Behavioral MCOs attempt to provide members with the names of several providers so they have a choice. Often MCOs set a maximum driving distance or a maximum time limit so members can access providers within reasonable distances from their homes. Sometimes, however, particularly in relatively small or isolated areas, there may be few providers with the needed expertise and competence. In such cases, MCOs may make special arrangements with patients to see providers. For example, the MCO staff may arrange transportation for a member. In other instances, the MCO may reimburse a provider who has the specific competency needed who ordinarily would not meet network standards. It is not uncommon for the MCO to even refer a patient to a nonparticipating provider, in order to access appropriate treatment services. The ability to provide a range of treatment services for members by accessing participating and managed-care-friendly providers who cover a specific geographic area continues to be problematic for many MCOs today.

## Provider Competence

Most behavioral managed care companies attempt to provide a range of provider competencies or skills within a given geographic location while attempting to monitor costs. The two major goals in establishing networks include securing services from the best, most competent and qualified providers and decreasing costs of a network over time (Shueman, Troy, and Mayhugh 1994). Both goals involve the use of criteria against which both provider competency and provider utility are measured. These goals, however, are often influenced by the specific characteristics of the member being served as well as by the geographic location covered. MCOs vary in terms of the amount of preparation, screening, selection and provider profiling they do. The strength of any network depends on the interaction of these factors in addition to the clinical skill of MCO staff such as case managers and utilization reviewers in guiding and educating providers in the MCO's specific treatment philosophies and accountability standards. This, as we will see, is no easy task!

In most cases, providers who are recruited as well as any providers who wish to join a network must fill out extensive paperwork and submit documentation of licensing and degrees. MCOs often interview potential providers, particularly large groups and staff at facilities, prior to making selection decisions. However, many MCOs realize that proof of licenses or degrees does not necessarily ensure provider quality or productivity. Nor does a less expensive provider guarantee cost containment. Network development is a highly complex task that requires ongoing refinement and modification if it is to be a strong, dynamic member-friendly system that is also cost-effective.

Typically, MCOs select and recruit providers with broad-based generalist competencies whose range of experience is extensive enough to allow them to deal with a wide range of patient problems. However, MCOs also recognize the need for specialists in specific areas. For example, the majority of therapists across the disciplines of psychiatry, psychology and social work have had clinical training in the treatment of depression; however, not all therapists are competent in such areas as pain management, eating disorders, or even substance abuse / dependence. Competencies are often addressed by determining what specific disciplines can do according to state licensing laws (Shueman, Troy, and Mayhugh 1994). For example, psychiatrists are set apart from other mental health disciplines in that they can prescribe medication by law. Another means of differentiating competency has to do with discipline-specific expertise. Generally, for example, doctoral-level psychologists are designated by most MCOs as competent to perform psychological evaluations and testing.

Provider cost is another factor that is considered carefully by MCOs when developing a network. Generally, contracted, or participating, providers have agreed to receive a preset reimbursement from the MCO for various services they deliver. For example, most mental health disciplines claim competency in some form of psychotherapy, although not all providers wish to perform this function. The participating provider has agreed to be reimbursed for psychotherapy by the MCO at a fee-for-service rate, which is generally discounted, in exchange for future referrals. Discounted rates tend to be, on average, 20 percent below market rates, or what is reasonable and customary. Unlike traditional, independent practitioners, participating providers generally realize less money per treatment; however, the payoff for the provider is a built-in referral system through the network. Of course, the number of referrals to a particular individual or institutional provider varies greatly, depending on that provider's competencies and adherence to the particular MCO's philosophy regarding treatment and its intensity, frequency, and duration. More significantly, however, most providers would report that the number of referrals received depends on other factors such as geographic location and availability of competing services and competing providers.

MCOs reimburse various disciplines differently. On average, psychiatrists are paid more per therapy hour than psychologists, who, in turn, are reimbursed at a higher rate than social workers, and so on. Different services are also reimbursed differently. For example, the average reimbursement for a psychiatrist contracted to do an expert consult is higher than reimbursement for a standard therapy hour. Likewise, the reimbursement for a medication follow-up is less than the reimbursement for a standard therapy hour. Various fees are set by the MCO for provider services rendered. These services can range from inpatient treatments to 20- to 30-minute therapy sessions, to phone consultations.

## BEHAVIORAL MANAGED CARE PROVIDER NETWORKS

Generally, networks employ some form of financial and administrative arrangement with providers. Many of the existing MH/SA service delivery systems utilized by behavioral managed care firms have been adapted from HMO models.

### The PPO (Preferred Provider Organization)

The base for most provider networks stems from concepts on which the PPO was formulated. Specifically, plan members, or subscribers, are motivated to utilize a set of preferred providers, both individual and institutional, by financial incentives or, rather, the structuring of the MH/SA benefit. Although there are many variations of this model, including the EPOs (exclusive provider organizations) and the POS (point-of-service) networks, the concepts of cost containment and consumer choice through the utilization of less costly, preferred providers are common even in the variations.

To become and remain competitive, behavioral managed care companies have utilized PPO concepts in their organization and management of MH/SA provider networks. Behavioral managed care companies have utilized such networks to service employer, union, and insurance carrier subscribers whose populations may extend over large regions and even the nation. PPOs are not individuals but rather service delivery systems through which unions, employers, and insurance carriers purchase mental health and substance abuse services for their members. The theory is that providers (individuals and institutions) will benefit by being part of the preferred network in that they will be guaranteed referrals over other nonparticipating providers. Generally, these preferred providers are paid at a negotiated (discounted) fee-for-service rate that is well below what is reasonable and customary. The out-of-pocket cost to the consumers of clinical service is less when they use a PPO provider instead of a provider who is not participating in the provider network. Although many plan members do choose non–PPO providers for many reasons, including familiarity with the provider or the area of provider expertise, the payer, such as the union, the insurance carrier, or the employer, will reimburse the member for less of the charges.

A critical rationale for utilizing a preferred network is the fact that behavioral MCOs, and thus the payers for whom the MCO is brokering services (through the establishment and administration of the PPO), have much greater control over the utilization of the benefits and cost containment. Essentially, the benefit design tends to drive service utilization toward the least costly provider (the PPO affiliate) (Winegar 1992, 51). By doing so, the payer, through the behavioral MCO, still offers the member a choice of providers and covers all medically necessary treatment, but at reduced utilization costs. Typically, using a PPO provider may entitle the member to 80 percent to 100 percent coverage/reimbursement, while utilizing a non–PPO provider may entitle the member to as little as zero to 50 percent to 70 percent coverage. Further, using a network provider, or utilizing the in-network benefit as opposed to the out-of-network benefit, will also relieve costs for members in terms of deductibles, maximum out-of-pocket expenses, and time spent in completing claims paperwork. Sometimes benefit plans provide further incentives by providing no coverage for specific types of treatment such as a partial hospitalization or an intensive outpatient program if the member chooses an out-of-network provider.

Behavioral MCOs who are enlisting institutions and facilities as a part of the preferred provider network generally contract with these entities to establish a per diem inpatient rate that is discounted from the rate of non–PPO facilities. For inpatient treatment, a per diem rate might be inclusive of both hospital and physician services. In some cases, however, the per diem rate for a hospital stay is separate from other charges. More recently, behavioral MCOs have utilized case rates with preferred, "core" providers to provide financial incentives for effective treatment planning and cost containment. The behavioral MCO is ahead financially in that members are guided toward less costly facilities. Given the choice, many plan members would opt for a hospital stay of $500 per day that was 90 percent covered by insurance with a $50 co-pay per day rather than a hospital stay of $1,000 per day that might only be 50 percent covered

**TABLE 2–1**

Sample PPO versus Non–PPO Benefits for MH/SA

| | Sample Benefit Structure: Mental Health/Substance Abuse | |
| --- | --- | --- |
| | **In Network (PPO)** | **Out of Network (Non-PPO)** |
| Deductible | $0 | $400 / $800 (individual / family) |
| Lifetime maximum | Annual maximum: $10,000 Lifetime Maximum: $50,000 | Annual maximum: $1,000 Lifetime Maximum: $10,000 |
| Hospital (IP) limits | None (Review for medical necessity) | 40 days per year 2 SA confinements per lifetime |
| Inpatient coverage (per admission) | 90% (after $150) | 70% (after deductible) |
| Outpatient coverage (per visit) | 90% (100% after $10 co-pay individual) (100% after $5 co-pay group) | 70% (after deductible) |

and involve additional out-of-pocket expenses and deductibles. Table 2–1 describes typical in-network and out-of-network differences in coverage.

As purchasers of MH/SA services become more cognizant of the role of risk-sharing and discounted fee-for-service rates in curtailing costs and utilization, many more PPO alternatives will be created and introduced (Lowman and Resnick 1994).

## Behavioral Managed Care Network Concepts

While in most traditional medical HMOs the primary care physician (PCP) is the "gatekeeper" of services (Winegar 1992), performing services personally or referring to specialists, in a behavioral managed care company this gatekeeping function is generally performed by the clinical staff. Goals of the MCO clinician include the quick assessment of risk of a particular member and subsequent preliminary treatment planning. The MCO clinicians can either perform this function, making an assessment regarding risk, impairments, and levels of treatment intensity needed, or direct the patient to an MCO network provider for further assessment, as in the case of a member who needs a psychiatric assessment to determine the need for hospitalization or one who requires a substance abuse evaluation prior to the determination of level of care.

One of the most significant means for providing quality care while containing costs is through the development of a strong network of mental health providers, as has been noted. By accessing the providers with the best competencies and the most clinically efficient practice patterns in various geographic locations, the behavioral MCO has succeeded in effecting access to quality and cost-effective treatment for its members/subscribers. However, the recruitment and hiring of providers is only one step in the process of creating a strong network. Such providers must also adhere to the behavioral MCO's philosophy and operations regarding brief, effective treatment. Further, these providers must be receptive to the ongoing case management and utilization review processes that are integral parts of the behavioral MCO's operation. Because a successful provider network requires much MCO hands-on effort in the shaping process, providers need to be made aware from the beginning that they are expected to work hand-in-hand with the MCO clinical staff in the process of reeducation, reevaluation and reclarification. Without the active participation and cooperation of network providers, neither the MCO nor the network will accomplish much in terms of quality of patient care and cost containment.

The recruitment of providers is necessarily a task involving the careful selection and screening of those providers who will best service the particular member/patient population in question. This process involves the accurate profiling of member/patient needs as well as the accurate profiling of provider competencies, productivity, and cost-effectiveness.

## Provider Selection

Depending on the parameters of the particular contract being managed by the behavioral MCO, such as geographic location and specific member characteristics, the selection of providers can be a very time-consuming and arduous task. For example, if the contract being managed involves a small number of members within a relatively confined geographic location, staff within the behavioral

MCO may be asked to supply specific provider contacts (Shueman, Troy, and Mayhugh 1994), whereupon a network is built gradually by word of mouth. However, in most cases the selection of providers is much more complex. Often companies must rely not only on commonly used community-based providers and provider groups but also on formal sources from which enough qualified providers from psychiatry, psychology, social service, addictions, and so on can be drawn. These sources include, among others, lists furnished by the APAs (American Psychiatric Association; American Psychological Association), the national register of health care providers, social work registers, and registers of marital and family practitioners.

Generally, providers who are selected to join a network must enter into an agreement with the behavioral managed care company in which they contract to provide services to a specific client group in exchange for a preset reimbursement schedule, which is generally a discounted fee-for-service rate. Providers must submit copies of earned degrees, licenses to practice independently, where appropriate, as well as at least three professional/personal references. Providers are also required to complete relatively extensive applications that request information about clinical specialties, populations treated, number of years' experience in different specialties as well as familiarity with treatment that is targeted and focused. It is not uncommon for a provider to be asked to furnish proof of expertise in specific clinical specialties such as the treatment of affective disorders and psychotic disorders. Often applicants must indicate the approximate number of treatment cases they complete in a typical month and the average number of treatment sessions per treatment episode they achieve. Providers are asked whether they will actively participate in case management and utilization review and whether they are available during crisis events. The specific treatment modalities commonly utilized by a provider, such as individual, group, marital/family treatment, are reviewed as well as professional liability coverage.

The provider screening, selection, and application processes attempt to determine the following:

1. Does this provider meet the minimum requirements in terms of licensing, certification, and professional liability coverage?

2. Does this provider have the necessary experience to treat particular patient problems, and is this provider familiar with at least minimum standards of accountability for treatment and treatment outcomes? Often providers with experience in specific systems such as VA and state hospitals and community mental health programs, are perceived as better choices because their experience, rightly or wrongly, has been in what many consider accountable systems (Shueman, Troy, and Mayhugh 1994, 57). Essentially these systems are reviewed by various surveying and accrediting bodies (e.g., JCAHO, HCFA, PA) and are also monitored by watchdog groups.

3. Are the specific traits and practice patterns of this provider in sync with the basic premises of the particular behavioral managed care organization?

For example, a managed care company may prefer providers who utilize alternative outpatient services such as group therapy or self-help organizations rather than those who utilize mostly individual therapy. A provider who has expertise as a generalist specializing in the treatment of illnesses such as anxiety or depression within certain patient groups such as adolescents or adults is more likely to be accepted on a network rather than a provider who simply indicates the specialties of sexual dysfunction or multiple personality disorders, which may be perceived as trendy and applicable to only a very narrow patient population (Shueman, Troy and Mayhugh 1994, 57). Further, providers who focus on brief, targeted treatment rather than highly intense and frequent voyages into self-discovery are preferred as are providers who perceive inpatient treatment as a last resort for an acute episode after having attempted other interventions. Providers who request specialized assessments such as psychological evaluation sparingly are preferred over those who routinely request ancillary services for purposes that are questionable.

After completion of the process of selection, screening, and review by the credentialing board, the provider is credentialed by the managed care company as a preferred, in-network service provider for that company. A contract is then executed between the provider and the managed care company. Generally, the contract specifies the professional obligations of both the provider and the behavioral managed care company, with particular emphasis on the handling of referrals, crisis events, and critical and adverse incidents. The contract also specifies the managed care company's guidelines regarding medical necessity of care as well as the role of the network provider vis-à-vis the MCO staff case manager and the MCO staff utilization reviewer. Such contracts address certification and precertification requirements as well as the provider's responsibility to comply with treatment planning protocols and telephone case review. Emphasis is placed on making the provider amenable to complying with the MCO's guidelines regarding treatment. To re-emphasize, most MCOs adhere to treatment in the least intrusive or restrictive setting with a focus on returning the patient to a functional level that is reasonable, not necessarily optimal (Shueman, Troy, and Mayhugh 1994).

The selection and credentialing of facilities and multilevel programs is done in essentially the same manner but with a different focus of scrutiny. From the start, many behavioral MCOs limit the types of programs and facilities they contract with, due to the extensive variations that may occur across programs. Different facilities may offer an assortment of treatment programs within their settings, such as inpatient treatment, partial hospitalization, intensive outpatient treatment, rehabilitation programs, residential treatment, and outpatient treatment. Licensed programs whose treatment philosophies adhere to the MCO's guidelines for medical necessity and who set clearly defined measures of accountability are preferred over those whose accountability standards are vague or minimal. It is for these reasons that many MCOs do not routinely contract with halfway houses or even some residential programs. Lack of consistency in programs and in quality standards pose multiple problems for MCOs in terms of accountability, treatment outcomes, and cost containment. Both programs within facilities as well as programs across different facilities that purport to treat the same member population, such as adolescents, vary considerably. These variations occur in licensing standards, in policies and procedures, and in basic philosophies. Differences are also evident in types and numbers of staff utilized, in staff credentialing, and in treatment planning, goals, and outcomes. Hence, MCOs must pay particular attention to what these program variations mean translated into financial outcomes such as LOS (length of stay), cost per treatment episode, treatment outcomes, and rates of recidivism.

## Provider Profiling

The process of provider profiling is integral to the success of behavioral managed care goals and is an ongoing process of redefinition and review. Provider profiling is the process by which the MCO reviews both process and outcome data regarding an individual or institutional provider to determine compliance with the overall clinical philosophy as well as the administrative parameters set forth by the MCO. These factors may include assessment of LOS in terms of frequency of therapy sessions or number of days in the hospital or in an IOP (intense outpatient program), number of adverse incidents (e.g., suicide, homicides) rate of return of treatment documentation, adherence to the medical necessity criteria of the MCO, cooperation with the MCO, particularly the case management and the utilization review processes, and receptivity to educational opportunities afforded by the MCO. Cooperation with the precertification process as well as cooperation with the denial of care process and the subsequent levels of the appeal process are variables that also may be monitored.

Provider profiling serves several functions, the most important of which include:

1. The weeding-out of poorer providers (individual and institutional) where utilization is consistently very high or where cooperation with the managed care process is found to be lacking, resulting in overutilization and inappropriate treatment.

2. The continued education of better providers in the philosophies and the ground rules of the MCO.

3. The identification of those providers whose performances indicate high patient satisfaction, low utilization, and high quality in terms of treatment outcomes and follow-up.

4. The continued education of the MCO regarding the identification of areas of expertise as well as geographic areas where provider resources are scarce or lacking and

where the MCO must expend its staff resources to foster better MCO–provider relations.

5.  The ongoing education of MCO case managers and utilization reviewers in clinically guiding providers towards patient outcomes that are successful for the patient and also cost-effective.

Both provider screening and provider profiling are still relatively new processes and continue to require much more empirically driven data collection and outcome studies. It is not always possible to alter or modify the performances of particular providers especially when they are part of a facility that is participating in a network but are not themselves participating providers in the network. The skill and level of expertise of the clinical staff who function as case managers and utilization reviewers have a significant impact on the provider–MCO relationship. Case management personnel, for example, who lack the necessary clinical skills and expertise to shape and work with providers may, in fact, drive costs up for an MCO in terms of number of therapy sessions or number of inpatient days, rate of recidivism, and utilization of inappropriate or unnecessary treatments. Further, less skilled MCO clinical staff may increase operating costs through the greater utilization of telephone time in order to complete reviews with providers.

Provider profiling, at the least, helps the MCO to eliminate the many poorer providers from the network, once identified through patient complaints or through the case management or utilization review process. In the case of institutional providers, many MCOs not only monitor basic clinical practice and outcomes, but often conduct actual on-site visits to assess the particular programs offered as well as the staff conducting the programs.

The process of provider screening and profiling is an ongoing process, determined in part by the degree of sophistication of the MCO. As the MCO increases in its clinical acuity, its demands regarding provider quality of performance tend to increase as well.

The process of developing a provider network that is effective for the patient, the provider, and the behavioral MCO is not without its difficulties. Key provider MCO problems are discussed in the next section.

# COMMON PROBLEMS AND SOLUTIONS IN PROVIDER NETWORKS

## Provider Cooperation with the Behavioral MCO

The process of establishing a strong, effective provider network is a two-way street between the behavioral MCO and participating providers. Cooperation with the MCO's goals and philosophy regarding clinical treatment as well as adherence to protocols for components such as precertification and concurrent reviews are necessary for good provider–MCO relationships.

Although the MCO may have utilized its best screening selection protocols to choose providers, often problems with particular providers are noticeable only months, or even years, after they have been operating within a network, depending on the number of actual patient cases they have handled. During the process of case management, for example, an MCO staff may identify a particular provider as problematic in terms of degree of cooperation with targeted, focused, brief treatment. The particular provider, even after education and mutual discussion of treatment planning with the case manager, may continue in his or her pattern of long-term individual therapy rather than opt for alternative treatments. Or it may become apparent during the utilization review of a particular patient's inpatient stay that the provider will not cooperate with the reviewer in returning phone calls. Providers may routinely refer calls to the UR (Utilization Review Department) of the hospital instead. It is also likely that patient reports may flag uncooperative providers. Commonly, a patient may call the behavioral MCO to report that a particular provider cannot see the patient for several weeks or that a particular provider is not working out for the patient. Often providers may fail to precertify treatment and only call when they are ready to submit a bill to the behavioral MCO.

Extreme solutions to lack of provider cooperation involve sanctioning a particular provider and removing the provider from the network. Less drastic solutions may simply involve review of the MCO's clinical philosophy and operations with the provider. In particular cases, referrals to a problematic provider may be put on hold pending a review of that provider's performance. However, often the solutions may not be simple, particularly in those geographic areas where providers are few and far between. In such cases, the MCO may choose to compromise with the provider in terms of the type and number of referrals generated, given the provider's resistance. At other points, the apparent lack of cooperation may be the result of ignorance or misunderstanding on the part of the provider. In these cases, the MCO may invest effort, time, and money in setting up educational seminars and meetings regarding state of the art treatment approaches to specific clinical problems. For example, many providers who treat sexual abuse often insist on having the patient delve into the past, thereby reliving the painful abuse experiences. In some of these cases, the patient may severely regress and require hospitalization. It is the clinical responsibility and in the best financial interests of the behavioral MCO to educate such providers in focusing on how the past history of sexual abuse relates to the here-and-now problems/impairments of the patient regarding issues of trust and revictimization.

Another related problem encountered by behavioral MCOs is the problematic provider who is a nonparticipating provider within a participating institution. MCOs must deal with particularly resistant providers in some cases who are not contracted with the MCO and who, therefore, are not responsible for adherence to any philosophy or treatment outcome other than their own. Often, after numerous unsuccessful attempts to enlist the provider's cooperation, the MCO's only recourse is to contact the hospital's administrator because the financial losses to the hospital due to this provider's disregard for precertification procedures or utilization review processes may become significant. Unfortunately, however, the MCO may have no impact on changing the behavior of the nonparticipating provider, even though the hospital or facility is a participating provider.

## Provider Identification of Patient Impairments and Treatment Goals

The key to most successful, targeted, focused treatment is the rapid assessment of risk, the identification of impairments to be fixed, and the formulation of treatment plans given the information provided. The roles of the clinical case manager and the utilization reviewer are critical to this task. Often, however, neither the behavioral MCO staff nor the provider are skilled enough to identify levels of risk, impairments, and treatment goals. This problem is frequently attributed to the fact that both the MCO staff and the provider may still be operating under the traditional premise of longer-term therapy without accountability for outcomes. The concept of managing mental health and substance abuse treatment may seem unachievable to them. It is at this critical point that MCO education of both providers and their own clinical staff may have its greatest impact on providing high-quality care while containing costs. The assessment of risk as well as the identification of impairments determines the treatment modalities to be utilized. Treating an individual for major depression without knowing his or her level of suicidality and the possible reasons for the depression or impairment to be fixed may unnecessarily prolong treatment and significantly hinder the patient from returning to his or her premorbid level of functioning.

### Provider Ability to Utilize Alternative Treatments

Another significant issue related to the degree of provider expertise and education in managed care treatment techniques and philosophies involves the tendency for many providers to automatically utilize such treatments as individual therapy rather than group therapy, or to automatically "step down" a patient from inpatient hospitalization to a partial hospitalization program (PHP) or to an intensive outpatient program (IOP). This inclination is not necessarily in the best interest of the patient. Often traditional PHP and IOP programs are simply prepackaged treatment programs with very generic goals and a specified number of mandated sessions of attendance that do not address needs of specific patients. These programs are frequently utilized as a default option in cases where the provider is unable for one reason or another to utilize or access alternative, more creative and individualized treatments. It is at this point that the case manager or the utilization reviewer can significantly impact the treatment process by suggesting such alternatives as outpatient therapy several times a week or in the case of a particularly vulnerable patient, a home health aid to prevent rehospitalization. As an important goal of behavioral MCOs is to return a patient his or her premorbid level of functioning and degree of independence as quickly as possible, it is imperative that the MCO staff intervene where appropriate, offering the provider options other than traditional programs that may be neither patient effective nor cost-effective.

## Provider–Behavioral MCO Communication

As behavioral MCOs become more sophisticated in terms of clinical jargon, clinical focus and clinical outcomes, providers in contact with MCOs have increasingly become more astute in their responses to MCO questions about patient care. Unfortunately, understanding the response needed to achieve certification for various levels of patient care does not necessarily mean understanding how to actually implement targeted, focused, least restrictive patient care. Frequently providers are well able to articulate the imminent risk of a patient in terms of suicidality (e.g., the patient plans to overdose and has access to prescription pills) or homicidality (e.g., the patient intends to use a gun on his stepfather when he comes home from work). However, they are often unable to describe participants leading to the imminent risk status of the patient (e.g., the patient was recently dumped by a girlfriend he had planned to marry) or the obstacles to patient wellness that have culminated in the current risk status (e.g., the patient fears that his wife will divorce him and he wouldn't see his kids). As a result, these providers often get stuck on questions and issues regarding implementation of positive patient change. For example, a provider may report that a patient is severely depressed and currently suicidal due to medication noncompliance. The MCO reviewer or case manager will proceed to question the why of the noncompliance because specific reasons may be uncovered that would determine the potential obstacles to wellness. Frequently, however, the provider may simply assume that the patient has little understanding of medications or the patient forgets to take the medication. In reality, the actual questioning of the patient and / or the patient's family or friends may bring to light the fact that the patient feels the medications are ineffective, or the patient is experiencing adverse side effects, or the patient does not have the money to purchase the medications. Once the specific reason(s) for medication noncompliance are clear, the provider and the MCO staff can work toward the goal of overcoming these obstacles to wellness. In this example, the provider may wish to reassess the medication, alter dosage levels, or enlist the aid of social services and the MCO to access the financial means to enable the patient to pay for the medications.

The process of effecting quality targeted and focused treatment requires much clinical skill, awareness of resources, and the utilization of alternative, sometimes more creative approaches. Both the provider and the behavioral MCO staff have much to learn from each other in making this process work.

## REFERENCES

Lowman, Rodney L., and Robert J. Resnick, eds. 1994. *The Mental Health Professional's Guide to Managed Care.* Washington, DC: American Psychological Association.

Shueman, Sharon A., Warwick G. Troy, and Samuel L. Mayhugh, eds. 1994. *Managed Behavioral Health Care: An Industry Perspective.* Springfield, IL: Charles C. Thomas Publishing.

Winegar, Norman. 1992. *The Clinician's Guide to Managed Mental Health Care.* New York: The Haworth Press, Inc.

# 3

# INSIDE THE BEHAVIORAL MCO

## OVERVIEW OF PRIMARY MCO FUNCTIONS

Although behavioral MCOs vary in terms of their specific department layouts and operations, they share several commonalities in terms of major functions. This common ground is directly tied to their mutual goals of high-quality patient care, in the least restrictive settings with cost monitoring and containment.

The primary functions of most behavioral MCOs include the following:

1. Clinical screening or gatekeeping and crisis intervention.
2. The referral process.
3. Ongoing reevaluation and modification of provider networks as well as the development of new networks.
4. The process of utilization management.
5. The process of clinical case management.

Secondary functions, which are extensions of primary functions in many cases or additional processes, may include the following:

1. Verification of eligibility.
2. Benefits analysis or interpretation.
3. Quality assurance or quality improvement.
4. Claims processing and payment.
5. Complaint processing.

6. Ongoing education of staff and providers.
7. Sales and marketing for new MCO–client business.
8. Medical records processing.
9. Management oversight and review.

For the purposes of this book, we will focus on the more integral functions.

### Clinical Screening or Gatekeeping and Crisis Intervention

This key function is generally served by the clinicians employed by the behavioral MCO as case managers, or care managers as they are known today, involved in either inpatient or outpatient case management or both. The significant aspect of this function is that it ideally is performed by a clinician, often known as a *gatekeeper*, who is competent to assess the level of risk or lethality and the immediate level of containment necessary to keep the patient safe. The gatekeeper, who generally works in conjunction with the provider, makes a careful determination regarding the intensity, frequency, and duration of treatment needed by a presenting member or patient. This process is integral to the MCO's goals of providing appropriate care while containing costs.

Inappropriate handling of this function can have major adverse effects on the quality of patient care, rates of recidivism, and treatment costs. For example, if a patient in crisis needing acute inpatient care is inappropriately referred to an outpatient program, the patient will likely represent within a short time for more intense services. If the accurate clinical assessment of risk had occurred, the patient might not have been inappropriately diverted to a lower level of care before being admitted to the inpatient setting. Also, the behavioral MCO would not have incurred the costs of two levels of care.

On the other hand, the clinical gatekeeper is frequently in a position to offer alternatives to more intensive and more costly care that may not be appropriate to the patient's level of treatment need. In such a case, the clinician can successfully complete a diversion from a higher level of care such as inpatient treatment to a more appropriate, less restrictive, lower level of care. A typical example would be that of an adolescent who is brought to the emergency room of a hospital after having a blow-up with his or her parents and threatening to run away. Admission to an inpatient setting for the purpose of preventing the adolescent from running away would be an inappropriate use of this level of care as well as an unnecessary restriction on the adolescent. The case manager might suggest linkage to an outpatient family therapist immediately. The manager may also suggest that the adolescent stay with a friend or relative overnight to enable the adolescent and the parents to cool down and address the conflict the following day. If the clinician is successful, he or she will have diverted the adolescent from a more restrictive and costly treatment setting, which was also clinically inappropriate, to a lower level of care. Attempted diversions that are unsuccessful are dealt with through a process of reviews and appeals that will be reviewed later in this chapter. Overall, the functions of clinical screening, gatekeeping, and crisis intervention ensure that recipients of care are accessing medically necessary treatment and not superfluous, duplicate, or inappropriate care.

## The Referral Process

The referral process is intimately linked to the screening and gatekeeping processes. The clinical case manager must make a rapid assessment of patient risk and based on the type of problem as well as the geographic location in which the patient lives, make a referral to a clinically appropriate level of care. Most behavioral MCOs have an 800 number with 24-hour access enabling members or clients to receive a referral at any time. Although most referrals are not the result of crisis situations, the MCO's ability to provide high quality patient care, while maintaining costs, hinges on the case manager's expertise and decision making. The need for clinical astuteness and common sense cannot be overstated. To make an appropriate referral, which by the way may include the names of several individual or institutional providers, the clinician must be well informed and well trained regarding the particular MCO's set of medical necessity criteria or practice guidelines. Further, the clinician must be able to quickly access both the benefit information regarding the eligibility of the member for specific benefits and the treatment allowances and restrictions stipulated by the member's plan.

Knowledge of a member's benefit plan is extremely important, particularly where benefits for certain types of treatment are excluded or are session-limited. For example, many benefit plans limit the number of outpatient sessions for a given contract year. Members are often unaware of the benefit restrictions. Hence, if a member's benefit plan offers only 10 inpatient chemical dependency days, of which the member has already utilized 6, the clinician must alert the hospital as well as the member regarding the remaining inpatient days that will be covered. Often, as part of the contractual agreement, the clinician must notify a hospital and/or a member that the provider being utilized is a nonparticipating provider. In many contracts, the member has the option to utilize a nonparticipating hospital or provider; however, the coverage is greatly reduced and may be only a fraction of the actual costs incurred. In this example, it is very likely that the nonparticipating facility, such as a hospital, will bill at a higher rate than a participating hospital that has already negotiated and contracted rates with the MCO. This means that the member, by utilizing a nonpar hospital, may be responsible for 40 percent to 50 percent of a $1,000 per diem rate, for example, in contrast to only being responsible for a small per diem co-payment or 20 percent of a contracted per diem rate of $550 by utilizing a participating hospital. Under some contracts, the member's use of a nonparticipating provider for a day treatment program or for an intensive outpatient program makes the member responsible for the entire cost of treatment as the benefit program does not cover any treatment costs rendered at a nonparticipating facility for those levels of care. Where possible, behavioral MCOs will attempt to negotiate a lower per diem rate with nonparticipating providers in order to reduce costs for the member.

Another important aspect of the referral process, particularly as it relates to referrals for outpatient treatment, is consideration of member variables. Member variables include the assessment of patient need for a medication evaluation in addition to a therapist, for example. The MCO clinician would assess this need in light of the member's risk status, the member's prior psychiatric or chemical dependency treatment, the member's support system, or lack thereof, and the member's willingness to accept a referral to a psychiatrist for medication evaluation. Further factors include the type of treatment being sought (e.g., family, marital, individual), the member's preference for a particular type of provider such as a male or a female therapist, a psychologist, a social worker, a marriage counselor, or an addictions specialist. The member's geographic location as well as ability to travel are also considerations in making an outpatient referral. Often, however, a member who is seeking help for himself or herself or for a family member does not know what type of treatment or therapist to request. The member must rely on the expertise of the clinician to make an appropriate determination of fit between the member and the network of providers. Most MCOs provide a member with several names of potential providers to contact. Although in some MCOs specialized "intake" departments consisting of nonclinicians may handle the more routine referrals, many MCOs are increasingly shifting to the use of clinicians or care managers to manage the mental health and substance abuse treatment benefits.

Although many members, once referred, continue to see the same provider, it is not uncommon for a member to call back and request names of additional providers. It is also very common that a member, once referred, simply chooses not to follow up with any therapist. Currently MCOs review this type of information to determine the actual utilization of a specific benefit, such as outpatient family therapy, in a particular geographic location with a particular provider or providers.

## The Provider Relations Department

This multifaceted department is integral to the operations of an MCO as it performs the key functions of building, reevaluating, and modifying provider networks. Further, staff employed in this area perform many other important functions related to network establishment and maintenance such as negotiating new contracts with providers, negotiating rates for treatment services rendered by participating and nonparticipating providers, gaining access to specialized services such as home health or VNA services and transportation. Provider relations staff frequently are responsible for informing both members and MCO staff of any changes in member contracts or in provider services. These departments keep statistical information on many aspects of provider functions including provider utilization and number of patient complaints about providers as well as provider complaints. Provider relations staff take corrective action where needed. Commonly, provider relations staff request information from other MCO staff about problematic providers to remedy situations, where possible. The provider relations department makes ongoing site visits to providers and attempts to attract needed provider services where they are minimal or lacking. This department handles the credentialing of providers and also frequently conducts in-services for providers. As was noted in Chapter 2, the development and maintenance of an effective provider network is very demanding if it is to adequately serve the basic goals of behavioral MCOs.

## The Processes of Utilization Review and Case Management

In addition to the formulation and upkeep of the network, the processes of utilization review, or as it is commonly known today, utilization management (UM), and case management (CM) are central and vital to the success of a behavioral MCO. These two functions can be perceived as falling along a continuum, depending on the degree of control and clinical responsibility utilized by the clinical staff. Traditionally, the process of UR was based on applying medical necessity criteria against levels of care retrospectively. However, the development of specialty behavioral MCOs has significantly altered this approach. Currently, utilization management, as it is more accurately described, is a very active process whereby the MCO clinician applies objective medical necessity criteria against patient levels of care such as inpatient treatment (IP), partial hospitalization treatment (PHP), intensive outpatient treatment (IOP), and outpatient treatment (OP), making a determination as to the appropriateness and efficacy of the requested or chosen level of care for the particular patient in question. This process actively involves the provider, the hospital, the member, the patient, and the patient's family, where appropriate, in the interaction with the UM reviewer or UM case manager. The current use of the utilization reviewer in the more clinically sophisticated MCOs is significantly more vital to the success of the MCO in terms of decreasing recidivism, providing the medically necessary level of care, and in containing costs. Utilization management, in essence, is a fundamental process intrinsic to effective case management. Currently, the use of the term "care manager" has been applied to those clinicians involved in reviewing patient cases.

The process of case management, which will be explored throughout this book, has often been viewed as requiring the greatest degree of clinical sophistication and expertise. Through the case management process, MCO staff actively direct, manage, and influence patient care in terms of linkage to providers, treatment planning, discharge planning, and crisis intervention. In many MCOs, the processes of utilization management and case management are often seen as intertwined, interdependent, and synonymous. Essentially, good utilization management is good case management. That is, both processes involve the active involvement of the MCO clinician in all aspects of care, from managing the initial intake to completion of care or successful aftercare planning. In some MCOs, a single clinician may perform both functions. However, the traditional distinction between utilization review and case management has been based on the financial weighting of the specific levels of care. For example, utilization case managers and reviewers have generally focused on managing and directing clinical treatment at higher levels of care such as in an acute care setting in hospitals, in a level of care that was part of a hospital or institutional setting, or in an alternative environment (e.g., custodial or residential arrangement). Oftentimes, the clinician whose focus was case management was perceived as managing care for patients requiring less intensive levels of treatment. This distinction is arbitrary and may be based on the number of treatment hours provided by a specific program on a daily or weekly basis. MCOs vary in their use of clinicians for the processes of utilization and case management. Similarly, MCOs vary in terms of what levels of care are considered inpatient and outpatient. Some behavioral MCOs include PHPs and IOPs under the traditional category of inpatient treatment, while others relegate these programs to the outpatient treatment category. Although these distinctions are arbitrary and are frequently cause for misinterpretation by provider facilities, the important distinction is derived from the degree or level of containment of risk or lethality, level of intensity of treatment services, and level of intrusiveness of patient monitoring. Additionally, the costs of these levels of care also vary, with acute care or inpatient hospitalization being the most costly.

# LEVELS OF PATIENT CARE OR DEGREES OF CONTAINMENT

Prior to describing the utilization review and the case management processes, it is important to have a working knowledge of the general, often arbitrary, distinctions in levels of patient care. They include but are not limited to the following categories, and many variations exist across behavioral MCOs.

## Inpatient Care, Acute Care, or Hospitalization

This level of containment involves the need for 24-hour psychiatric and/or psychiatric/medical patient monitoring and supervision. This monitoring is generally performed by nurses and aides with the attending physician (AP), usually a psychiatrist, making daily visits and visits on an as-needed basis in the case of an emergency or patient crisis. Depending on a specific patient's circumstance, the psychiatrist may enlist the aid of a physician specializing in internal medicine, addictions, and so on to aid in treatment planning and patient problem-definition and resolution. For most behavioral MCOs, this level of care, IP, is utilized in those cases where the patient poses an imminent risk to himself or herself, to others, or to property or where the patient is so psychiatrically disabled or compromised that he or she is unable to perform even basic life-sustaining functions such as eating and staying out of harm's way. This level of care is also utilized in cases where the patient is imminently in need of medical detoxification. Examples of medically necessary uses of inpatient hospitalization are admission of a patient who has just overdosed or who is actively planning his or her suicide and has verbalized a specific plan. A patient who is actively verbalizing homicidal ideation, intent, and a specific plan and who has the means (e.g., a loaded gun, a knife), would also be an appropriate candidate for this level of care. An individual who presents in the emergency room (ER) as intoxicated and who has a history of alcohol-related seizures or whose vital signs are severely elevated or depressed would also be admitted to this acute level of care. As we will see, however, the medical necessity for this level of care is not always as clear as the examples given. The inpatient level of care is generally the most restrictive level of containment, as well as the most costly. Hence, many behavioral MCOs tend to review the medical necessity of inpatient care every few days. The focus of the MCO case manager is to work with the primary provider in identifying and reversing or containing the problems of the patient that necessitated this level of care so the patient can move to a less restrictive, more independent level of functioning as quickly as possible.

## Residential Treatment

This level of containment is also highly restrictive and requires 24-hour monitoring; however, the type of monitoring is different from inpatient or acute care in that the patient is not considered in acute crisis. In this situation, the patient requires ongoing monitoring and supervision for the purpose of providing a living arrangement in which treatment can be provided. Often the focus of the MCO case manager is not on reversing patient problems but on providing a safe and structured environment for a patient who cannot successfully be treated in the home environment. This type of treatment is not a covered or fully covered benefit under many mental health and chemical dependency benefit plans. If any treatment is covered by a benefit plan in such an environment, the MCO generally manages only the medically necessary treatment, which might be the equivalent of a PHP, an IOP, or OP. Under most benefit plans, the member or family is held responsible for all other costs, such as room and board, as residential treatment is perceived as a type of placement option over an extended period of time. Frequently patient problems necessitating this level of care are not perceived as curable or reversible in an efficient and expeditious manner. Change is perceived as occurring over a much longer, sometimes indefinite period of time. This type of care setting is perceived as a custodial arrangement and is utilized in cases where the patient's family is unable to adequately provide a safe living environment or safely contain the patient at home. Recipients of this level of care might include conduct-disordered adolescents with coexisting psychiatric and/or substance-abuse problems or the chronically mentally ill patient who simply cannot function outside this structured supervised setting.

## Partial Hospitalization Programs or Day Treatment

This level of containment is utilized in cases where a patient may not need the intensive structure of an acute setting or a hospital admission but requires substantial monitoring, treatment, and supervision due to the potential for risk or lethality. Most PHPs operate five to seven days a week, often six to eight hours, and sometimes twelve or more hours a day. Patients engage in group and individual treatment with clinicians and/or addiction specialists and see their physician, usually a psychiatrist, once weekly. In some cases the psychiatrist may make daily visits. Most PHPs are distinguished from inpatient levels of care in terms of number of treatment hours, risk potential, and need for supervision and monitoring. PHPs may cover daily treatment but not 24-hour treatment and supervision.

Often the PHP is utilized, rightly or wrongly, as a step-down from inpatient treatment. Currently, however, this almost automatic progression has been met with criticism by MCOs as well as by providers who feel that alternative, less restrictive levels of care can be appropriate for patients discharged from acute settings. Where applicable, a patient may receive certification for medically necessary PHP treatment in a variety of configurations. A patient may require only three days of PHP a week, or maybe seven days a week. Generally, a PHP is treatment for a predetermined number of hours per week but under 24 hours a day. It is significant to note that an institutional provider, such as a hospital or an agency, determines the medically necessary level of care per patient by using its program goals as a standard, whereas a behavioral MCO determines the medically necessary level of care through its criteria or practice guidelines.

## Intensive Outpatient Treatment

Similarly, this level of containment is differentiated from other levels of care in terms of risk status, degree of supervision, and number of treatment hours. Admission to this level of care requires the determination of a patient's level of risk and need for structured supervision. The IOP has been utilized as an automatic step-down from the PHP. Again, this almost automatic transition has received much criticism. The distinction between IOP and outpatient treatment is somewhat difficult for most case managers reviewing for medical necessity care. Entry to an IOP is determined by the risk status and individual needs of the patient in question. In most cases, the patient engages in individual and group treatment under the supervision of a clinician or an addictions specialist and sees the attending psychiatrist or physician once a week or, in some cases, each day the patient attends the IOP. Generally, IOPs run three to four hours a day and may be conducted during the day or in the evening. Treatment in an IOP setting may also occur in a variety of configurations, based on what is deemed medically necessary treatment for the particular patient. Frequently, IOPs are utilized in cases involving chemical dependency.

## Outpatient Treatment

This level of care is generally the least restrictive and least intensive. It is also the least costly, although there are exceptions depending on the types of services rendered as well as their frequency and duration. OP levels of care are distinguished from IOPs in terms of risk level and number of hours as well as in the need for monitoring and supervision. Outpatient services may involve multiple hours of treatment per week but are seen most frequently as treatment once to twice weekly. The patient may be engaged in individual and/or group treatment depending on specific patient needs. Outpatient treatment often involves therapy in combination with medication management by a psychiatrist. The outpatient therapy may involve family treatment, marital treatment, treatment involving school personnel or employers, as well as individual treatment.

## The 23-Hour "Hold" Bed

This level of treatment is utilized, where possible, in cases of crisis where it is determined that 24-hour inpatient treatment may not be medically necessary. However, patient observation is necessary for a period of time to rule out or rule in admission to an acute inpatient care setting. The 23-hour hold bed gives staff, generally emergency room staff, the time to evaluate a patient and the patient's access to support, such as family and friends, without immediately admitting the individual to an inpatient unit. Although the 23-hour hold bed is not found at every institutional provider, it is frequently utilized in cases where a patient can be talked down from a crisis situation and where the patient will contract for safety and has the support of family and friends until he or she can receive treatment at the appropriate level of care. Often a crisis team contracted by the hospital or behavioral MCO may be utilized to make a thorough assessment of patient risk. Commonly, a 23-hour hold bed may be utilized in cases where a patient requires observation due to his/her intoxicated state. In some cases, patients may return home in 23 hours or less after being medically cleared. The use of 23-hour hold beds involves significant clinical skill in determining the current and potential risk of the patient.

Although behavioral MCOs will vary in their determinations of which level of care is medically necessary for a particular patient, given the specific practice guidelines, these divisions in types of care are basically standard in their progression in terms of patient risk and degree of containment and treatment required. As we look more closely at the process of case management, including utilization review, we will look at specific patient factors and variables such as impairments or obstacles to wellness.

## UTILIZATION REVIEW AND CASE MANAGEMENT: THE INTEGRAL LINK

Current utilization review, or utilization management, unlike traditional utilization review, is a much more active, dynamic, and evolving process whereby the clinical case manager becomes an integral player in patient care. The case manager advocates for the patient by overseeing and directing patient care with the participation of the primary provider of the care. In essence, the case manager manages the provider to ensure only medically necessary care for the patient in the least restrictive and intrusive setting. The focus of the case manager is to return the patient to as great a level of independence or autonomy as possible, as quickly as possible. Effective clinical case management significantly impacts utilization rates of different levels of care and different types of services as well as rates of patient recidivism. Ideally, such case management allows patients easy access to appropriate levels of care where treatment will reduce, contain, or overcome obstacles to mental health and wellness and, at the same time, reduce unnecessary, duplicate costs of patient care. Naturally, the reality of case management is frequently different from the ideal given the various players in this process.

Having been a primary provider, as well as an MCO inpatient and outpatient case manager and, thus, having experienced both sides of the coin at different times, I have been amazed at just how sophisticated and at times difficult the actual processes of UR and CM can be. As such, I offer the following points that I have observed as critical in making the process work for my colleagues, both primary providers and MCO clinicians, as well as for patients.

## Critical Factors to Effective Utilization Review and Case Management

### Understanding the Role of Case Management in Mental Health and Substance Abuse and Substance Dependency Treatment

Unfortunately, clinical case managers within MCOs are often in adversarial positions with primary providers whose cases they are managing. This has been attributed to the bad press associated with behavioral MCOs as well as to nonacceptance, anger, and even fear on the part of some providers. Primary providers often perceive MCO case managers as the enemy ready to deny patient care and hence detract from their livelihoods at the drop of a hat. MCO case managers, particularly those with limited expertise, may rigidly adhere to the literal interpretation of medical necessity guidelines, thus often sacrificing sound clinical judgment. Just as case managers are perceived as quick to deny care, providers are often perceived as quick to utilize unnecessary and inappropriate care or to overutilize services. Although there certainly are both providers and MCO case managers who fall into these categories, the majority of mental health professionals, both within MCOs and serving patients as primary providers, are working towards the common goal of high-quality patient care.

### Common Communication

One of the most critical impediments to effective UR and CM for both the primary provider of care and the MCO case manager is the failure to use a common language to convey information. The fact is that behavioral managed care utilizes its own unique communication system. Most of us who have been providers for any length of time can certainly answer the questions asked by MCOs; however, we have frequently not asked or answered the questions that are commonly asked.

MCO communication, which is largely based on behavioral terminology (e.g., observable, objectifiable, quantifiable events, people) attempts to quickly capture the *what,* the *why now,* the *how,* and the *who* of treatment. This method of communication and information-gathering attempts to focus the provider as well as the MCO case manager on providing the highest quality patient care in the least restrictive setting while maintaining costs. The following key concepts are critical to understanding and actively participating in the CM and UR processes.

### Medical Necessity Guidelines

Medical necessity guidelines vary from MCO to MCO; however, common to most of them are:

1. The concept of a validated DSM-IV diagnosis. This means that a diagnosis has been established, even tentatively, based on the standards and specifications set forth in the most recent Diagnostic and Statistical Manual of Mental Disorders (currently, DSM-IV).
2. The concept of risk—as imminent or nonimminent and the degree of containment needed to manage the level of risk presented.
3. The degree of impairment of the patient in level of functioning.

*Imminent Risk and Nonimminent Risk:* Although each behavioral MCO has its own unique set of medical necessity criteria, most, if not all, initially and concurrently assess the level or degree of clinical instability or patient risk. Level of clinical instability or risk determines the level of containment or treatment setting required to ensure the safety of the patient, as well as the safety of other individuals. If they are to be effective, medical necessity criteria or guidelines must be clinically sound and must take into consideration the patient as a whole entity in the here and now. Biological, psychological, social, and cultural factors are all important in determining level of risk, care setting, treatment course, and discharge planning and linkage.

Generally, the concept of clinical instability or degree of lethality is assessed in terms of temporal proximity and probability of:

1. Self-harm.
2. Harm to others/property.
3. Inability to care for self, placing self and/or others at risk, and inability to perform life-sustaining functions (due to organic factors, psychosis, etc.).
4. Medical complications from substance withdrawal or detoxification.
5. Medical complications/psychiatric complications as the result of treatment (e.g., electroconvulsive shock treatment (ECT), meds).

The level of risk may range on a continuum from imminent risk (e.g., an immediate risk for self-harm or harm to others within an immediate time period, usually 24 hours or less) to moderate risk (e.g., may have suicidal ideation weekly but is in control of thoughts and actions) to no risk (no suicidal ideation).

As most mental health professionals are aware, the level of risk of a particular patient is often very difficult to predict, even with past history of risk behaviors or lack thereof. Because risk is so difficult to assess, MCO case managers or care managers will often zero in on the precipitant or the why and now of the patient's problems. Although the precipitating event to a patient's needing treatment is significant to the course of treatment, this concept must also be accompanied by questioning the meaning of the precipitant for a particular patient. For example, a job loss or a divorce may have quite different meanings to two different patients, necessitating treatment for one and not the other. The precipitating events, the meaning of these events, and the biological, psychological, social, and cultural context in which the patient functions will all impact the level of risk, the level of care setting, and the course of treatment as well as discharge and aftercare planning.

### Critical Impairments or Obstacles to Wellness or Improvement

For the provider and the MCO case manager to formulate a targeted, focused treatment plan for a patient, they must first agree on the identification of specific patient impairments or problems that need to be reversed, overcome, altered, or contained in some observable way. Patient problems that are generally addressed first are those requiring immediate treatment planning and intervention such as suicidal ideation with a plan and the means, homicidal ideation with a plan and the means, or severe alcohol withdrawal resulting in highly elevated vital signs. In such cases, treatment planning would involve attempts to stabilize the patient's mood and medical condition first. Less critical and non-life-threatening problems might also be addressed during the course of treatment; however, the patient may well require a lower, less intense, less intrusive level of care once imminent risk is no longer present. Both the level of risk or lethality identified and the types of behavioral impairments or problems identified will help to determine the particular treatment planning for a patient within a given level of care.

In most MCOs, reviews are conducted not only prior to or at the point of admission to treatment but also concurrently during the course of treatment. Concurrent reviews serve to aid both the provider and the case manager in reassessing risk and in reassessing patient problems and concurrent treatment plans for their efficacy and efficiency. Traditionally, patients might have been certified for days or even weeks and months of treatment at a time; however, managed care's focus on only medically necessary, targeted, focused treatment has led to concurrent reviews that are often conducted every few days. Although providers complain about the intensity of the case management process, this process has served to reduce and curtail unnecessary, highly restrictive and often costly patient containment and treatment. Concurrent reviews of patient progress and treatment planning more clearly define what the provider is accomplishing or not accomplishing during treatment. At certain points, it may be necessary for the MCO case manager to intervene and recommend alternative treatment plans, levels of care, treatment services, and treatment modalities.

### Treatment Modality
Treatment modality is understood to mean the *how* of accomplishing specific treatment goals. These modalities may include psychopharmacology, ECT, individual and group therapy, VNA services, expert consults, family and marital treatment, and so on.

### Discharge Planning and Aftercare Linkage
Discharge planning and aftercare linkage are integral concepts to effective case management in terms of maintaining a patient in the most clinically appropriate and least restrictive setting while also decreasing the likelihood of recidivism. Although discharge and

aftercare planning begin at the time a patient is admitted to treatment, these concepts are frequently the last to be considered by providers as well as by MCO case managers. One of the most frequent criticisms leveled by MCO case managers is the seeming inability of providers to adequately plan for and implement patient aftercare. Commonly, both individual and institutional providers request assistance from MCO case managers in linking patients to appropriate aftercare treatment settings and placements. Traditionally discharge planning was often left to the nursing or social services departments within institutions or agencies without much input from the primary provider of services. However, MCOs are increasingly attaching greater significance to the integral role of providers in treating the patient on a continuum from admission through discharge. In fact, concurrent medical necessity criteria often include a requirement for having an established discharge / aftercare plan in place early on in the course of treatment.

In summary, the basic concepts underlying medical necessity criteria, risk assessment, patient impairment, treatment planning, treatment modality, and discharge linkage must be openly discussed and understood by the provider and the MCO case manager to promote a healthier, more patient-centered approach by both parties.

### The Noncertification Process

Frequently disagreements arise between a provider, a member, a patient, a patient's family, and the MCO case manager regarding the level of care or treatment type that is considered medically necessary and will be approved or certified. A common scenario is that in which a provider wishes to continue inpatient treatment for a patient who is no longer presenting imminent risk. In such a case, the provider may indicate that the patient could still benefit from a few more days of acute inpatient hospitalization for the purposes of stabilization. In this example, the case manager may decide that the patient could benefit from a less intrusive level of care, as the patient no longer meets the medical necessity criteria for continued stay in the inpatient setting. The case manager has the following options:

1. Suggest a lower, less restrictive level of care such as a PHP, an IOP, or outpatient treatment with support or ancillary services (e.g., VNA or home healthcare, psychotherapy).

2. Proceed with the noncertification process whereby the case is reviewed by an outside party, who is generally an independent contractor for the behavioral MCO, in conjunction with the attending provider for the patient's case.

Depending on the outcome of the request for noncertification, any of the parties involved may request an appeal of the initial decision made by the MCO's outside reviewer. In most MCOs, there are several levels of appeal, and in some there are clinical management and grievance committees that reexamine cases against medical necessity criteria. The noncertification process as well as the levels of appeal allow input from outside reviewers, thus affording the patient even greater clarification and scrutiny in terms of the appropriateness and the quality of the care they are receiving. Of course, there exist many variations in the noncertification and appeals processes and some MCOs even conduct immediate on-site reviews with the primary provider of care. We will review actual examples of utilization review, noncertification and the appeals processes in certain examples in the next several chapters.

## BASIC TENETS OF CLINICAL CASE MANAGEMENT

Although utilization review and clinical case management vary across behavioral MCOs, certain guiding tenets or premises appear to be common to most operations. The tenets on page 63 reflect overall philosophies of behavioral managed care companies, that is, the focus of behavioral MCOs is to ensure high-quality, medically necessary patient care in the least intrusive and restrictive setting, while containing costs.

Knowing the basic operations and language of utilization review and case management does not, however, lead to good case manager/provider rapport, nor does it lead necessarily to good case management. Two examples serve to illustrate well the criticisms leveled by primary providers and MCO case managers about each other. (See Example 1 and Example 2.)

Example 1 clearly indicates the possibility of treatment failure when one party devalues the contribution and clinical integrity of another party's judgment. The MCO clinician in this case became

1. Medically necessary treatment is not always medically desirable treatment.
2. *More* treatment is not necessarily *better* treatment.
3. Imminent risk is frequently determined by examining motive, means, and opportunity.
4. Patient safety takes priority over any financial considerations regarding treatment.
5. The case management process does not dictate treatment; rather, it involves careful clinical oversight of patient care by the case manager in conjunction with the primary provider.
6. Discharge planning begins at the time of patient admission to treatment at any level of care.
7. Accurately determining level of risk involves a high degree of expertise and clinical skill.
8. Do not assume the provider knows and agrees with the specific medical necessity criteria utilized by a particular behavioral MCO.
9. Education of both the MCO case manager and the primary provider by each other is integral to effecting high quality patient care.
10. Many providers are not in sync with the philosophy and principles of behavioral managed care. The case management process exists to ensure the highest quality patient care in the least restrictive setting while containing costs. It is not about being popular.

trapped in his own biases regarding the provider's agenda and he based his reviews on the literal interpretation of criteria without exercising sound clinical judgment. The clinician also inappropriately attempted to restrict this patient's access to a needed level of care. Had the psychiatrist not had the conviction to pursue the more appropriate course of treatment, the clinician's negligence and extremely poor judgment might have had quite adverse consequences for the patient.

Example 2 illustrates the very significant impact that lack of provider responsibility and accountability have on treatment, as

## Example 1

Take the case of the 42-year-old female who was admitted after a suicide attempt via an overdose of prescription pills. She had been hospitalized once before for a suicide attempt precipitated by the loss of a family member. She had a family history of depression as well as a history of being abused and was diagnosed with major depression. The provider, her psychiatrist, had been treating her on an outpatient basis, intermittently, over many months, during which time she had made no suicide attempts, appeared to be adequately dealing with her problems, and was compliant with antidepression medication.

The psychiatrist and MCO case manager agreed that the patient's high-risk status necessitated an inpatient admission for crisis stabilization. The psychiatrist responded to questions about the patient's impairments by suggesting that she appeared in part to suffer from a biological depression for which he would reevaluate her medications, as well as from psycho-social stressors that had exacerbated her depression. The patient had experienced many recent losses, including that of a job, and she was currently facing bankruptcy. She was a single parent, with little social support, who felt unable to supervise and control her 12-year-old child. The last straw for this patient had been the recent breakup with her boyfriend.

The psychiatrist agreed to treat her daily to focus on loss and trust issues, realistic problem solving, and ways to access community social and financial support systems. He also wanted to try her in a PHP for a few days in order to provide additional support. The MCO clinician disagreed with the psychiatrist's suggestion of a PHP to ensure patient stability because the clinician perceived the inpatient admission as being adequate to this task. More significantly, the clinician thought that most PHPs were a waste of time and money and were usd by only poor providers as a default option. The clinician had independently concluded that the patient was simply personality-disordered and was acting out to get attention and to escape her problems. He disagreed with the diagnosis of major depression and felt the provider was inappropriately concerned about this patient's level of risk. The clinician, drawing on written practice guidelines of criteria, determined that the PHP was not medically necessary. According to this clinician, outpatient treatment was the only correct treatment modality and PHP was a red flag for inappropriate treatment.

*Continued*

---

**Example 1, concluded**

Though the psychiatrist held his ground, the clinician continued to perceive the psychiatrist as missing the boat and as avoiding real patient issues. In a final attempt to convince the psychiatrist of his error, the clinician offered home health services for the patient; however, this provider declined, stating that without a few days of intensive structure as well as intensive individual therapy, no amount of home health services would prevent the patient from either decompensating and requiring another inpatient admission or, worse, committing suicide. According to the psychiatrist, the real issues of trust, abandonment, and revictimization needed to be directly confronted within a safe, supportive environment. Exasperated by the provider's perceived resistance and lack of cooperation with managed care guidelines and criteria as he understood them, the clinician sent the noncertification request for PHP to an outside physician reviewer who reviewed the case with the psychiatrist. The case was subsequently certified for PHP on the basis of meeting medical necessity criteria.

---

well as the importance of appropriate identification of patient problems and precipitants leading to establishing a therapeutic course of treatment. The provider in this case became adversarial and ultimately refused to address family conflicts. His antagonism toward both the MCO clinician and the MCO process blindsighted his ability to exercise sound clinical judgment and problem solving, resulting in unnecessary complications. Instead of focusing on patient issues, he attempted to gain control over the review process, as well as support for his position by making the MCO the enemy.

As we will see in later chapters, improved communication, understanding, and shared patient responsibility will foster a greater balance among high-quality patient care, cost containment, and professional growth and autonomy for both the provider and the behavioral MCO case manager. The success of effective case management is very much tied to a positive working relationship between the primary provider of care and the MCO case manager. It is only with the ongoing education of the provider by the MCO, and the MCO by the provider, that this outcome can be achieved.

## Example 2

Alternatively, take the example of a 13-year-old female admitted to an inpatient psychiatric unit with an electrolyte imbalance due to not eating. She had lost 20 pounds over two months, which was significant for her 5′ 3″ frame, and the provider feared cardiac arrhythmias as a result of the imbalance. The provider diagnosed her with anorexia nervosa. During discussions with the MCO case manager, the psychiatrist indicated that he wished to stabilize the patient's physical condition and then transition her to a lower level of care. The provider reported that he was unaware of any immediate precipitant to this patient's hospitalization, except her medical condition, for which he was considering tube feeding. The case manager suggested a medical, rather than psychiatric hospitalization, with both individual and family therapy on a daily basis while the patient was inpatient. She continued to probe the precipitating event. The provider flatly refused the suggestions made and stated the patient required an inpatient psychiatric setting to deal with her psychiatric problems.

At this point, the clinician questioned the provider about the patient's psychiatric problems and recommended that the provider bring the patient's family in for a discussion of possible contributing factors. The psychiatrist, irritated by the clinician's recommendations, indicated that he had already seen the patient's parents and her sister, and he reported no family problems. He indicated that the patient had a distorted body image and that she was also depressed. Dissatisfied with these responses, the MCO clinician asked the psychiatrist to identify observable obstacles to the patient's well-being that needed to be treated, overcome, or held in check in order to reference a lower level of care. The psychiatrist, quite angry at this point, indicated that he simply wanted to stabilize the patient's physical condition with medication and food monitoring and would then discharge her.

On the fourth day of review, the psychiatrist reported that the patient was stable, physically, but after hearing that she would be discharged home, she had threatened suicide on the unit. He advised the MCO case manager that he could not ethically discharge the patient at this time. Of course, given the imminent risk of the patient, the MCO case manager certified the inpatient stay as it met medical necessity criteria. Even so, within an hour, the clinician received a phone call from the patient's father who was outraged. He had just been informed by the facility that his daughter's inpatient stay might not receive further certification from the MCO.

# 4

# CHARACTERISTICS OF CASE MANAGEMENT

## THE MANAGED CARE MODEL OF TREATMENT

The rise of brief, focused, and targeted treatment that is medically necessary across an individual's lifespan is integral to managed care oversight of patient care.

### Outpatient Treatment

Typically, MCOs utilize clinical staff to case manage treatment either across the continuum of a treatment episode from inpatient to outpatient care or with inpatient and outpatient case management separate functions performed by different clinicians. In many of the more sophisticated MCOs, significant emphasis is placed on the outpatient case management process due to its relationship to higher levels of care. Specifically, appropriate outpatient treatment can significantly reduce rates of recidivism as well as prevent patients from needing higher levels of care. Unfortunately, some MCOs still do not place enough clinical emphasis on outpatient treatment and may inadvertently increase costs and decrease quality of care through their lack of scrutiny of outpatient reviews.

The managed care model of treatment is significantly different from traditional forms of psychotherapy and the characteristics of providers of each are also quite different. Prior to reviewing these differences, it is important to note that outpatient treatment carries different definitions depending on the MCO and the providers utilized. For example, in some MCOs, outpatient treatment may encompass a PHP or an IOP. However, other MCOs may stipulate outpatient treatment to be a specific number of hours per week below the level of a PHP or an IOP. In many cases it may involve therapy once weekly, while in other cases it may involve six or more hours of treatment per week. The specific treatment modalities for outpatient treatment may include individual, group, family, marital, or couples therapy as well as medication management or some combination of these modalities. Further, outpatient treatment may involve additional services such as outpatient ECT, home health services, phone consultations, and expert reviews. The many variations found in outpatient treatment are the means for ensuring the best fit for a patient to maintain the least intrusive level of care and prevent both entry and recidivism to higher levels of care, where possible. Often MCOs will automatically offer patients some form of outpatient follow-up, even in cases where higher levels of care have been found not to meet medical necessity criteria.

## General Characteristics of Treatment

In differentiating managed care treatment from more traditional therapies, the points discussed in the following sections are significant.

### Medically Necessary Treatment versus Medically Desirable Treatment

Whereas in traditional therapies an individual could choose to enter a course of treatment to enhance his or her inner growth and self-understanding, or even to satisfy court-ordered recommendations, MCOs certify only medically necessary treatment. Medically necessary treatment is treatment aimed at quickly reducing or alleviating the obstacles or impairments for which a patient initially sought treatment. The impairment is seen as requiring treatment if there is some level of clinical instability apparent (e.g., the patient is not at high risk for self-harm, but the risk may increase if the patient is not treated at this level of care). Treatment may also be required if there is some degree of impaired functioning at home, at work, or socially (e.g., the patient's level of depression is causing the patient to miss work or the patient's obsessive-compulsive behavior is causing the patient to be late for work or social engagements). There also must be a validated DSM-IV Axis I or Axis II diagnosis whose symptomatology must be the focus of treatment or which places the patient at risk. Hence, patients having Axis II personality disorders would receive treatment if they also had an Axis I diagnosis of major depression, for example, whose symptoms were the real focus of treatment or a diagnosis that places them at risk or if the Axis II diagnosis, by its symptopsychology, placed the individual at risk of self harm or harm to others. Generally speaking, managed care treatment would not include treatment that might be medically desirable, such as self-actualization therapy, growth therapy, or different types of experimental therapies because these therapies are not deemed absolutely medically necessary to the well-being and functioning of the individual. Exceptions, of course, exist.

### Targeted, Focused Treatment

Unlike traditional therapies, most MCOs require the formulation of treatment and discharge planning on entry into treatment. The treatment planning document, which is completed on admission to treatment as well as concurrently through the course of treatment, must be individualized to the specific patient, must contain identified obstacles to wellness, or impairments, and must also indicate treatment goals that are observable, achievable, and behaviorally based. For many providers, achieving a managed care appropriate treatment plan that also includes a discharge plan is an ongoing learning process.

Traditionally, providers have had free reign in the formulating of goals for treatment and in judging when these goals were met. Often patients were in treatment for years with therapists who attempted to cure the patient of all maladaptive problems and behaviors. Currently, managed care treatment models that require greater provider accountability for patient outcomes have forced providers to scrutinize the what and the how of treating patients. The goal of curing the patient, although it may occur, is not the driving goal of managed care treatment. Instead, managed care providers attempt to focus on the problem(s) that brought a patient into treatment initially. MCOs focus on the here and now of patient problems and attempt to return the patient to his or her prior level of autonomy and independence as quickly as possible. Unlike many traditional therapies, treatment within the context of managed care does not attempt to focus on the past or rewrite history. Nor does it attempt to cure all pathology. In contrast to traditional therapy goals that are often vague and relatively unachievable, MCOs are demanding outcomes of treatment that are tangible and observable. For example, a treatment goal could include the return to employment within two weeks by a patient or compliance with taking medications for seven days. Goals such as increasing self-esteem or decreasing anxiety are simply no longer acceptable without demonstrations of actual outcomes. Neither does giving medications for the sake of stabilizing a patient serve as an acceptable goal without specifying what outcomes will be observable and tangible as a result of taking medications. Essentially, will the medication effectively limit obsessive-compulsive behaviors such that the patient is able to get to work on time five days a week?

### Brief, Intermittent Treatment across the Lifespan
Unlike traditional therapies, managed care often assumes that the patient who seeks treatment is motivated to change and is an active player in therapy along with the therapist. It also assumes that most individuals, through the course of their lifespans, may need treatment interventions for brief periods of time to overcome impairments and return to their prior levels of independence. Hence, much of the patient change occurs outside the therapeutic setting in the present and in the future. The therapist is perceived as a catalyst during the episode of treatment. Traditional therapy often assumed that any patient change occurred through the therapist and that most patients had to be cured regardless of their degree of motivation or degree of awareness of their problems. Many traditional therapies were seen as very significant and critical in the patient's life and patients were often in therapy several times a week over the course of several years. Unlike traditional therapies, managed care models do not assume that there are preferred modalities of treatments such as individual therapy. Rather, MCOs use any and all, often nontraditional resources within the community to effect patient change.

### Present-Centered Therapy
In contrast to traditional therapies that tend to explore history and past relationships as they relate to a patient's current mental status,

managed care therapy tends to focus on current maladaptive behaviors and utilizes a patient's history only as it is relevant to current behaviors. Traditional therapies, for example, often attempt to delve into the memories of victims of sexual abuse, sometimes reawakening vivid, nightmarish recollections in patients. In contrast, current managed care models would consider the trauma of past sexual abuse relevant only in as much as it related to the patient's current feelings regarding trust, abandonment, and revictimization. Additionally, traditional approaches to chemical dependency and abuse often involved programs lasting 28 days or longer. Current managed care therapies focus in large part on safe medical detoxification or social detoxification, with a return to a lower level of care as soon as possible. In some instances, even PHPs and IOPs are seen as too intensive and too intrusive a level of care for chemical dependency treatment alone. Much literature has generated support for self-help groups such as AA and NA as being equally, if not more, effective than day hospital or intensive outpatient treatment.

### Treatment as a Therapeutic Intervention Rather than as a Cure
Many traditional therapies have perpetuated the concept of cure as the most significant goal of the therapy process. Proponents of the MCO model of brief, targeted, and focused treatment have suggested that such a concept is, in itself, self-defeating. Rather, therapy is simply a therapeutic intervention across a patient's lifespan. Proponents of the managed care model of therapy assume that most individuals who seek treatment want help in dealing with typical problems and crises that occur within the human condition. These problems or crises would include such events as the death of a loved one, divorce, illness, loss of job or economic security, or loss of a child. Unlike traditional therapies whose focus was on curing a patient of all maladaptive behaviors and negative concepts held within the conscious and the unconscious, the managed care model attempts to identify typical response patterns that have been used by an individual during problematic times or crises and help the individual learn new coping strategies as quickly as possible. Most growth occurs outside the therapy setting where the individual learns to utilize these new coping strategies. Each therapeutic intervention across the lifespan serves to build on preceding coping skills to adapt to new crises or problems in human development.

## Characteristics of the MCO Therapist or Provider

Of significance to many professionals as well as to many behavioral MCOs are the specific characteristics of therapists who work well within the managed care environment. Although there are a multitude of traits that differentiate the managed care therapist from the traditional therapist, the following are the most salient.

**1. Rapid Problem Solving and Focus**  The therapist questions the precipitant to the patient's seeking help now and what significance that precipitant or event or person has to the patient.

**2. Delineation of Observable and Achievable Goals**  The therapist and the patient are active participants in treatment. After patient obstacles or impairments are mutually identified, the patient and therapist must agree on goals to achieve during treatment. These goals must be practical and achievable for the patient.

**3. Therapy Begins During the First Session**  In contrast to the history taking and information gathering performed by traditional therapists, managed care therapists attempt to involve the patient immediately. History that is relevant to the presenting problem is utilized, but patient history in general may be gathered throughout the course of treatment.

**4. Both the Patient and the Managed Care Therapist Are Active Players**  The patient is encouraged to do assignments and utilize new coping skills outside the therapy session. The therapist and the patient alike are responsible for their input and motivation. For example, one criterion often utilized to gauge whether or not treatment is medically necessary is the patient's progress as well as the patient's compliance with mutually established treatment goals.

**5. No One Treatment Method or Modality is the Best**  Therapists use whatever modality will be the most effective for a particular patient. In some cases, that may mean utilizing family therapy in conjunction with self-help groups or a home health aide in conjunction with individual therapy. Active participation in community support and self-help groups is strongly encouraged.

Some basic assumptions of providers endorsing the managed care model of treatment include the following:

1.  A patient's return to treatment is not necessarily a treatment failure.

2.  Therapy and change occur largely within a developmental continuum across the lifespan.

3. There is no perfect therapist for a given patient.

4. Cure is not necessarily the goal of therapy.

5. Practical and focused therapy makes the most effective use of time. Therapy is not limited to a 45- to 50-minute hour, since the process of change generally occurs outside the therapist's office.

## CASE MANAGEMENT OPERATIONS

Clinicians within MCOs serving the role of case manager perform a variety of functions. First, many times a patient will call in crisis and will require immediate assessment for risk and safety factors. Second, a patient may call needing more routine treatment, at which point the clinician must also determine the risk level and the level of patient care required. Third, an individual or an institutional provider may call to review the specifics of patient cases and to request further certification. In all these scenarios, the case manager plays an integral role. Case managers perform various other functions as well.

### Case Management and Crisis Intervention

Regardless of the behavioral MCO in question, most MCOs have clinicians on call over a 24-hour period of time, enabling patients access to care at any point. Many MCOs utilize designated clinicians on staff during the day as the clinician on call, and they may provide an 800 number allowing patients access to clinicians after routine business hours. This structure ensures ready access to treatment and crisis intervention for a patient. In assessing a patient in crisis, the case manager must work quickly to make a determination of the patient's degree of lethality. The questions on page 74 are a sample of those questions often utilized in assessing a crisis situation.

The experienced MCO case manager can readily assess the severity of risk and possible options for treatment even by asking a few of the questions indicated. Providers are encouraged to ask the same questions when dealing with a patient as well as when handling less emergent or urgent traditional treatment situations. During a crisis, the case manager must make a decision regarding the level of containment necessary to keep the patient safe. It is not uncommon for a case manager to attempt to talk a patient down from

1. Is the patient suicidal? Does the patient verbalize a plan? If so, does the patient have access to the means?

2. Is the patient dangerous to others? Does the patient verbalize a plan to hurt somebody else? Who? What about duty to warn?

3. What is the patient's past history? Of suicide attempts? Of violence towards others or property?

4. Is the patient hallucinating? If the patient is hearing voices, what are they telling him/her to do?

5. Is the patient evidencing paranoid delusions? Delusions of any sort? Such as a delusion in which the patient feels he is a bird and can fly off any building?

6. Is the patient so psychotic as to be incoherent? Unaware of the environment? Could the patient place himself/herself in risky situations? How risky?

7. Is the patient's impulsivity likely to place him or her in harm's way without outside intervention.

8. How old is the patient?

9. What are the identified support systems for the patient? Family? Friends? Therapist?

10. Where is the nearest emergency room? How can the patient be transported to the emergency room as quickly as possible? Ambulance? Family? Paramedics? Police?

11. Should the police be called to assist in the situation?

12. Should the patient be kept talking on the phone while help is called?

13. What resources are accessible to the patient today? At this hour?

14. Can the adolescent stay overnight at a relative's or friend's house until a family conflict can be resolved?

15. Is the patient using alcohol? Drugs? If so, how much? When was the most recent use?

16. Does the patient require detox due to medical complications? How high/low are the vital signs? Is the patient at risk for seizures? For DTs? Does the patient require observation? Can the patient be detoxed outside of an inpatient acute setting?

17. Is the patient on medication? If so, what kind? For what?

18. Are there any medical conditions that complicate the crisis? (e.g., Hypertension? Diabetes?, etc.)

self-harm or harm to others while attempting to send help to the patient. It is also not uncommon to call on the police, fire department, or even the sheriff's department or paramedics in the area to assist during a crisis.

## Case Management in Non-Urgent Treatment Situations

In general, however, most MCO case managers will handle less urgent situations and will deal with the primary providers of care rather than with individual patients. This is true for case managers who handle higher levels of care such as inpatient treatment and for case managers who handle lower levels of care such as outpatient treatment. Regardless of whether a case manager is reviewing inpatient or outpatient treatment, or both, the same questions regarding risk are posed, this time to the providers of care.

Typically, the process of case management for higher levels of care is less scheduled and more frenetic than for lower levels of care. This is due to the fact that urgent or emergent situations generally involve phone calls to case managers as emergencies arise. In contrast, case managers reviewing lower levels of care are often able to schedule telephone reviews with providers at specified times. What is often obvious to an observer entering an MCO is the difference in activity level of case managers, depending on the level of care being managed.

The significance of outpatient case management cannot be overstated, although it often appears to play second fiddle to the more intense, financially driven utilization review and case management of inpatient treatment. It is significant that outpatient intervention may occur at any point along the continuum of care for a patient. That is, a patient may start in an outpatient setting and require admission to a higher level of care later. The patient will, at some point, be stepped down again to outpatient treatment. Additionally, a patient may first enter treatment at a higher level of care and eventually move to lower, less restrictive levels of treatment. It is also true that outpatient treatment may be provided even within a higher level of care. Although the process of managing the provider and the treatment in an outpatient setting may appear less intense and less frenzied than case management for a patient in a hospital setting, the process requires a high degree of clinical skill, experience, and assertiveness on the part of the MCO case manager.

Keeping in mind the various characteristics of managed care therapy as well as the characteristics of managed care therapists, the outpatient case manager has a challenging task to perform. While case managers managing providers and patient treatment at higher levels of care deal generally with physicians and UR/UM departments, outpatient managed care case managers must deal directly with professionals from all mental health and chemical dependency backgrounds. These include both participating and nonparticipating professionals. Outpatient case managers often must communicate with their own colleagues who frequently downplay the role and the significance of outpatient case management. Noteworthy is the fact that many patients who were traditionally treated at higher levels of care can, today, be successfully managed in an outpatient setting given skillful management by the MCO case manager.

## TIPS FOR CASE MANAGERS AND PROVIDERS

In order to successfully engage in the case management process, both case managers and providers need to be willing to learn from each other. Communication using a common language is especially helpful in bridging the gap between an MCO clinician and a primary provider of care. Tips for both MCO case managers and providers are offered on the following pages to make the most effective use of case management for the patient in question.

## Tips for MCO Case Managers

1. Know your company's client contracts. Although this may not be your area of expertise, you will invariably be asked questions about them. Specific contracts may have specific limitations in terms of treatment levels and types for a contract year.

2. Do not assume that all providers are familiar with managed care principles or operations. Time spent on giving information to providers is time well spent for the success of case management.

3. Know where your backup is in case of a crisis situation.

4. Become familiar with the geographic locations of your providers as well as the availability of community resources in these areas.

5. Your job is to manage patient treatment effectively and to provide direction to the provider. Keep a therapeutic distance when it comes to the clinical arena.

6. Do assertively manage the patient treatment plan as well as the provider's handling of the case where appropriate.

7. When unclear about the specifics of treatment, request clarification from the provider.

8. Offer suggestions and alternatives to treatment where appropriate. Providers, like case managers, may not be aware of alternative treatment modalities or options.

9. When in doubt about a clinical issue, discuss it with the provider and seek other opinions from colleagues.

10. Try to flag high risk cases that will require more intense case management.

11. Suggest a medication evaluation where appropriate.

12. Attempt to educate the provider on your company's policies, medical necessity criteria, and paperwork demands.

13. Do try to be available to providers by phone.

14. Make certain that you, yourself, understand the questions you are asking providers before asking them.

15. Become familiar with the other departments within your company in order to direct non–case management questions to appropriate departments as quickly as possible.

## Tips for MCO Providers

1. Precertify treatment with your case manager.
2. Become familiar with the MCO's criteria for medical necessity.
3. Become familiar with the noncertification and the appeals processes.
4. Be able to identify the precipitant, event, or person, etc., that has caused the patient to seek treatment now, versus at any other time.
5. Identify the meaning or significance of that event, person, etc., to the patient.
6. Identify the patient's real agenda for coming to treatment.
7. Determine what the mutually agreed upon goals for treatment are.
8. Be able to identify patient problems and impairments and observable goals to overcome or reduce these impairments or problems.
9. Make sure goals are achievable.
10. Identify what will determine the end of treatment for the particular patient.
11. Determine what treatment modalities will be most effective for the patient.
12. Determine whether you intend to involve family members, friends, employers, etc.
13. Determine whether the patient may require medication in addition to therapy. If so, bring this to the attention of the case manager.
14. Determine whether the patient is complying with the treatment goals. If not, try to determine why not. Determine whether or not the goals should be reevaluated.
15. Determine what types of homework, if any, are appropriate for the patient.
16. Determine whether the patient can utilize additional community resources. If so, which ones can you suggest?

*Continued*

**Tips for MCO Providers, concluded**

17. If treatment is not progressing, determine whether or not you are contributing to the problem. If so, consider whether you need to refer the patient to someone else. Consult with your case manager regarding options.

18. Determine what the discharge and aftercare plans of the patient are.

19. Estimate how many days or sessions you will need to successfully complete this episode of treatment.

20. When requesting more days or sessions, be prepared to give a sound rationale for the request.

21. Make sure you know how the particular MCO handles crises. If not, ask your case manager as you may encounter such a situation.

22. Know what the protocol is in the event of an adverse incident (suicide, homicide, etc.).

23. Determine whether or not duty to warn is warranted.

24. Know when you need a consult with an expert. Ask the case manager for a referral.

25. Know whether appropriate releases of information have been signed by the patient.

26. Become familiar with particular treatment plan forms (admission, concurrent, and discharge) utilized by a particular MCO.

27. When unsure, utilize your case manager for information, both clinical and administrative.

28. Follow up on questions to which you do not have the answers.

29. Be aware that if you are unable to reach your case manager, you can usually access the clinician on call.

30. Remember that you and the case manager will not always agree on the management of patient treatment. Agree to disagree at times.

# 5

# CASE MANAGEMENT OF MENTAL HEALTH AND CHEMICAL DEPENDENCY
## *MCO Case Manager and Primary Provider Interactions*

$P$rior to reviewing case scenarios, the reader is encouraged to bear in mind the various goals of case management in mental health and chemical dependency treatment, as well as the limitations to case management oversight. Noteworthy is the observation that, regardless of the information available to case managers and providers, the processes of case management and utilization review, with their specific sets of clinical practice guidelines or medical necessity criteria, continue to remain a mystery to many, including reviewers themselves, providers and recipients of care. At this point the reader is advised to view utilization management as integral to overall case management. At some points in the text the terms case management and utilization management are used interchangbeably. The use of the term "case management" alone necessarily includes the process of utilization management.

This section is intended to clarify the actual processes for the reader by drawing on typical case scenarios from the simple to the more complex. It is by no means the absolute or correct way of reviewing but is intended to allow the reader a feel for the case management process as well as a feel for what the provider typically experiences during the process. As will be seen, the concepts of medically necessary treatment, imminent risk, precipitant, and the meaning of events are actually very sophisticated. Unfortunately, many providers as well as case managers fail to see the significance in reviewing and understanding these concepts. However, behavioral MCOs realize that only by targeting the precipitant, the meaning attached to the precipitant, the degree of risk, and the obstacles to improvement can effective treatment from intake to discharge be rendered.

## GOALS OF CASE MANAGEMENT IN THE TREATMENT OF MENTAL HEALTH AND CHEMICAL DEPENDENCY

The following goals, although not exhaustive, are among the major hallmarks of MCO case management.

1. To provide medically necessary treatment, which is not necessarily the same as medically desirable treatment.
2. To provide treatment in the least restrictive and the least intrusive environment while ensuring the safety of the patient as well as the safety of other individuals.
3. To utilize any and all treatment modalities to provide medically necessary treatment in the least restrictive environment.
4. To educate providers, reviewers, and the public on the meaning and significance of effective provider–MCO interaction and dialogue during the case management process.
5. To utilize all necessary adjunctive or additional resources such as expert consults and home health care to ensure medically necessary treatment that is appropriate to the patient in question.
6. To maximize treatment benefits by identifying obstacles to the patient's well-being that require immediate and longer term intervention thereby reducing the frequency of unnecessary patient recidivism.
7. To work collaboratively and collegially with provider(s) in the treatment process.
8. To creatively, as necessary, utilize all appropriate community resources to enhance patient treatment.
9. To serve as an active deterrent to treatment that is not medically necessary or is inappropriate, duplicate, or detrimental to the patient's health by utilizing the MCO's

clinical criteria or guidelines in conjunction with providers to assess the quality of treatment being rendered. Because clinical disagreements will arise, it is also the goal of MCOs to provide a series of outside checks and balances through a series of appeals and grievance processes.

10. To provide targeted, focused treatment that is outcome-based.

Naturally, case management of mental health and chemical dependency treatment also has several limitations. The following reflect the significant limitations, although these also are not exhaustive.

## LIMITATIONS OF CASE MANAGEMENT IN THE TREATMENT OF MENTAL HEALTH AND CHEMICAL DEPENDENCY

1. Medical necessity criteria or practice guidelines continue to require greater refinement in terms of objectivity and quantifiability, as well as greater consensus by case managers, providers, and the community on what constitutes medically necessary treatment.

2. Lack of clinical expertise and sophistication continue to make the application and the understanding of medical necessity guidelines problematic.

3. The scarcity of broad-based, comprehensive provider education regarding clinical principles and operations of MCOs continues to thwart optimal treatment and to create potentially adversarial relationships among providers, case managers, and recipients of care.

4. Poor communication and misunderstandings between MCO case managers and providers continue to place patients in the middle of case manager–provider controversies.

5. Provider networks continue to require ongoing review and scrutiny, such that providers who are opposed to, or lacking in knowledge of, managed care principles involving provider accountability and outcome-based patient treatment are weeded out from managed-care-sensitive providers.

6. Existing community programs that are unable to provide medically necessary, outcome-based patient treatment require reexamination and redefinition if they are to continue to service patients effectively.

7. Improved treatment options must be developed and utilized to ensure the provision of optimal care for chronic patient populations.

8. Aftercare and discharge planning must be perceived as integral to the treatment process and not merely as an afterthought pieced together prior to actual discharge.

9. College, graduate school, and medical school curricula need to incorporate areas of study in the philosophy and implementation of behavioral managed care principles.

10. Outcomes studies, including comparison studies, regarding effective and noneffective treatments and treatment-related variables require continued exploration. These studies will enhance the understanding and implementation of those variables enhancing treatment efficiency and treatment quality.

## OVERVIEW OF THE CASE MANAGER–PROVIDER INTERACTION

In this section the reader will review several typical clinical examples involving the management of treatment by the MCO. As will be noted, some examples are more common than others; yet all attempt to reveal the importance of direct and open communication between the primary provider of care and the MCO case manager. These examples also reveal the fact that although providers and case managers may be quite clinically competent, determining medically necessary care by accurately identifying precipitants, patients' perceptions, and patients' impairments is a much more complex task than it first appears. Lastly, it is apparent, in some of the examples, that fear, ignorance, lack of clinical sophistication, or a combination of these factors and others may quickly create an adversarial relationship between the provider and the MCO case manager. The ensuing power play often serves to the detriment of good patient care.

The following scenarios are meant to serve as examples of typical MCO reviewer–provider interactions. These examples are intended to demonstrate the significance of identifying patient risk, the precipitant or proximal cause to a patient seeking treatment, the why now or the specific meaning of the precipitating event to the patient, the formulation of the treatment plan based on the identification of patient obstacles to wellness, and the formulation of the discharge and aftercare plan. These factors, in turn, will foster ongoing treatment intervention and support thus, optimally, decreasing the frequency of patient relapse and recidivism.

The examples also attempt to reveal how medical necessity criteria is applied to specific cases. Assessment of risk as imminent or life threatening, as potentially life-threatening, or as routine is examined. Other criteria including the patient's ability to cooperate and comply with treatment, the patient's prior treatment history, and the patient's current support systems are examined. The patient's ability to benefit from one level of care versus another and the patient's need for structure are considered. Careful aftercare planning cannot be overstated; however, it will be noted that this factor is frequently the weakest link in the clinical process for numerous reasons. Most commonly, the provider's lack of clarity in assessing the critical issues of patient risk, precipitant, significance of precipitant, and patient obstacles to wellness hinder the provider's ability to plan for discharge and aftercare. In essence, if the focus of treatment is simply that of stabilizing and discharging the patient without a clear awareness of the events or factors leading the patient to treatment initially, it is probable that the patient will again return for similar treatment in the near future.

Clinical astuteness in the identification of specific patient variables requiring treatment is the cornerstone of effective case management in terms of treatment and discharge planning. This approach serves to create a truly individualized patient treatment plan from intake to discharge and aftercare.

Unfortunately, many providers as well as case managers perceive these treatment questions as unnecessary and time-consuming, particularly with the noted financial pressures inherent in the mental health care industry today. With ongoing education of providers and MCO case managers, it is the belief of proponents of behavioral managed care that an individual patient may be provided with the optimal treatment necessary to return to a prior level of autonomy as quickly as possible. By exacting a targeted and focused treatment and aftercare plan, MCO proponents suggest that a balance will be achieved between treatment efficacy and quality and treatment cost.

# INPATIENT CASE SCENARIOS
## Example #1

A 45-year-old male has been brought to the emergency room by a friend who has just found him at home with a loaded gun. The patient told his friend that life was not worth living any more because his wife was going to leave him. The patient had no prior history of psychiatric treatment, was not on any medication, and had no history of substance abuse or dependency.

Provider X, a psychiatrist, is requesting inpatient admission for this man due to his imminent risk for suicide. The patient has the means, a gun, and appears intent on harming himself.

Provider X and the MCO case manager probe the precipitant or the proximal cause of this patient's desire to kill himself. According to the patient's friend, the patient's wife had threatened to leave the patient a few days prior to this event.

Both the provider and the reviewer agree that the patient is imminently, that is, immediately, at risk for self-harm and the precipitating event is the wife's threat to leave. Both the reviewer and the provider must now determine the meaning of this event to the patient that resulted in his need for this acute level of intervention. The meanings attached to specific precipitants will determine the particular patient's problems that require treatment. Provider X communicates that he will attempt to stabilize the patient by prescribing antidepressants and will discharge the patient to a partial program for a few more days of stabilization and structure.

Reviewer Y communicates to the provider that stabilization, although immediately necessary, is only one aspect of the patient's treatment. The following dialogue is typical of provider–case manager discussions.

*Reviewer Y:* We have identified the threat of the wife's leaving as the immediate precipitant; however, is this the first time the wife has threatened to leave? What does this really mean to the patient? It seems that with the patient's permission, his wife might be willing to participate in a marital session. What do you think?

*Provider X:* Look, the patient has a suicide plan and he also had access to a gun. I don't know anything else about the patient as I've just seen him for the first time. I do know that he's still talking about shooting himself and he's too high risk for me to send home.

*Reviewer Y:* This case meets the medical necessity criteria for inpatient treatment because of the patient's imminent risk status, and I will clinically certify a day until you and I can discuss the case further when you have more information. As you know, the more we can understand about what triggered such an extreme event on the patient's part, the better we can determine the treatment and aftercare plan.

### Day 2—Concurrent Review

*Provider X:* The patient is still talking about killing himself, and he will not contract for safety. I spoke to his wife, and she is willing to come in and talk. Apparently she has threatened to leave several times before, but this time she actually filed for divorce with a lawyer. This really has hit home for the patient.

*Reviewer Y:* Did you ask the patient what he feels or perceives about his wife's leaving him?

*Provider X:* Yes, and it seems that the patient perceives the loss of his wife as meaning that he is worthless and no good. He thinks he will never be lovable and never find anyone else to be his partner. According to the patient, life is not worth living because he is nothing and has nothing without his wife. These were the patient's own words.

*Reviewer Y:* You seem to have clarified why this patient wanted to commit suicide. In addition to the medication management, what other interventions do you plan to include in treatment? For example, individual therapy could be utilized to help the patient cope with the loss of his wife and his perceptions about himself as a result of the impending divorce. Does he have any other support systems such as family or friends? Can we access them to help the patient cope during this crisis?

*Provider X:* I've already scheduled a marital session for today and his close friend, the one who brought him here in the first place, is willing to come in if the patient agrees. I think that participation in individual therapy will also help the patient to deal with his feelings and understand how his beliefs and perceptions are impacting him.

*Reviewer Y:* Medication and supportive therapy are appropriate; however, when will you know that the need for an inpatient acute treatment setting is over? What is the treatment plan for discharge and aftercare?

*Provider X:* As soon as the patient is no longer verbalizing a plan to kill himself and is willing to contract for safety, I'll transition him to a partial program for a few days.

*Reviewer Y:* Are you sure that the patient will require the level of intensity inherent in a partial program? Why not set up an intensive program including individual treatment with a therapist, medication management with you, and refer him to a community support group? There are many self-help groups that deal with the trauma of divorce.

*Provider X:* Well, I just thought it would be a natural progression from inpatient to PHP. We generally transition patients to the next lower level of care.

*Reviewer Y:* As you know, the goal of treatment is to provide only medically necessary treatment in the least restrictive and least intrusive setting. This patient needs support during this crisis, that may be better provided in an outpatient setting with people who are undergoing similar crises. However, if you decide to pursue the partial program, we will have to review the case to determine whether or not medical necessity criteria are met. In the case of this patient, the real potential for self-harm must be present. Further, the patient's condition must warrant that level of structure and supervision provided by the partial program. The question is what you intend to treat or to reverse or to change in the partial program that could not also, and perhaps more appropriately, be dealt with on an outpatient basis.

## Summary of Example #1

### Imminent Risk Criteria for Inpatient Acute Psychiatric Hospitalization: MET

◆ Patient had a plan to shoot himself and had possession of a gun. (Depending on the particular MCO, the patient's statement of suicidal intent may be sufficient to warrant certification.)

### Identified Precipitant or Trigger

◆ Wife threatened to leave and filed for divorce with a lawyer.

### Identified Meaning of the Precipitant

◆ Patient felt he was worthless without his wife and he might as well be dead.

### Obstacles to Wellness

◆ Patient has numerous problematic beliefs or misperceptions about himself; patient feels worthless and unlovable; patient feels he will never find another mate.

### Treatment Plan

◆ Biological intervention: antidepressant medications.
◆ Psychosocial interventions: marital therapy, individual supportive therapy to help patient deal with his erroneous beliefs about himself.

### Discharge Plan

◆ Linkage to psychiatrist for medication management.
◆ Individual therapy.
◆ Community support groups to help patient cope with divorce.

## Example #2

A provider calls the MCO to precertify the admission of a 35-year-old male to an acute inpatient psychiatric unit. This male was brought to the local hospital by staff from the group home at which he is residing. Staff report that the patient is evidencing bizarre behaviors, is increasingly paranoid, and is responding to voices. He has verbalized that the voices have told him his medications have been poisoned by staff and he must kill his roommate who is part of the conspiracy to murder him. The group-home staff also report that the patient has been increasingly self-isolating and hypervigilant and has been hoarding things in his room. On inspection, staff have found numerous sharp objects that they have confiscated. The request for psychiatric admission was the result of a recent physical attack on his roommate during which he cut his roommate on the back of the neck. His roommate required stitches as a result.

The patient has a 15-year history of schizophrenia and has lived in various sheltered and protected environments most of his adult life. He has had six prior inpatient admissions, all of which included similar symptomatology.

The provider and the reviewer agree that the criteria for inpatient admission has been met, due to the immediate risk for homicidality, secondary to the paranoid delusions and command hallucinations associated with the schizophrenic episode. However, as the patient had not needed acute psychiatric treatment in over five years, the question of the trigger to his psychotic episode requires understanding and clarification.

Provider X determines from discussions with the group-home staff that the patient's roommate, who is relatively new to the group home, had complained about the side effects of his medication to the patient and to the staff. Both the provider and the reviewer hypothesized that medication noncompliance was a distinct possibility. Prior to the recent episode, the patient's symptoms had been well controlled by antipsychotic medications. The provider agreed to have blood levels drawn to determine the validity of the hypothesis. The patient was placed on antipsychotic medications and nursing staff monitored closely for compliance. The reviewer agreed to clinically certify the patient for acute treatment until his psychotic symptoms remitted and he no longer posed an immediate threat to his roommate or to others.

As the patient's psychotic symptoms diminished, the provider was able to determine by questioning the patient directly that the patient, indeed, had stopped taking his medications, fearing that they were poisoned. He had heard his roommate constantly complain about the medications and the patient, himself, became obsessed with the idea that his own medications were poisoned. Of course, the vicious cycle began since the patient's noncompliance with medications essentially precipitated a psychotic break, that in turn escalated his paranoia, eventually causing him to act violently.

The major obstacles to wellness, the paranoid delusions and command hallucinations, were treated primarily through a biological intervention: antipsychotic medication. Additionally, the provider and reviewer agreed that continued education for the patient about his illness and about his need to take medication could be accomplished through outpatient group therapy. The reviewer also recommended increased training for the group-home staff in monitoring for medication compliance and in the management of problem behaviors in their population of chronically mentally ill individuals.

## Summary of Example #2

### Imminent Risk Criteria for Inpatient Acute Psychiatric Hospitalization: MET

+ Patient was a homicidal risk to his roommate secondary to the schizophrenic break that included paranoid delusions and command hallucinations telling him to kill his roommate.

### Identified Precipitant or Trigger

+ Patient stopped taking his medications that resulted in his attack on his roommate in response to psychotic symptoms.

### Identified Meaning of the Precipitant

+ Patient's roommate had complained about side effects of his medications and this patient stopped taking his own medications. This resulted in an exacerbation of schizophrenic symptoms including paranoid delusions and command hallucinations.

### Obstacles to Wellness

+ Noncompliance with medication because the patient feared the medications were poisoned. Need for closer monitoring by group-home staff of medication compliance and potentially dangerous behaviors. Patient's lack of understanding of his illness.

### Treatment Plan

+ Biological intervention: antipsychotic medications.
+ Psychosocial interventions: group therapy to educate the patient about his illness and about the importance of taking medications.
+ Educational support of the group-home staff in monitoring for medication compliance and in the management of chronically mentally ill patients.

### Discharge Plan

+ Return to group home.
+ Medication monitoring including blood levels as necessary.
+ Ongoing group therapy regarding medication compliance.
+ Reconsideration of placement of patient with another roommate.

## Example #3

Provider X, an ER physician, calls to notify the reviewer that he has just admitted a 16-year-old male to an inpatient psychiatric unit because the male is allegedly a danger to himself and to his parents and is at risk for running away from home. The patient has a history of crack use since age 14, has had numerous legal run-ins including attempted robbery, and has been involved in many physical fights with peers. He is currently failing most school courses and has been repeatedly truant. Just prior to the admission, the patient had a fight with his parents over the use of the car and threatened to run away. The patient's parents, who were overwhelmed by the situation, decided to bring him forcibly, with the help of the police, to the hospital emergency room.

Provider X reported that the patient was a danger to himself and to others due to his impulsivity and his plan to run away from home. Reviewer Y confronted the provider about the patient's imminent risk and questioned whether the patient was actively suicidal or homicidal. Provider X denied any suicidality or homicidality but insisted that, although the patient had not verbalized any intent or plan, the provider still felt that the patient required inpatient treatment to calm him down.

Reviewer Y proceeded to question the inpatient treatment plan and he was told that the patient required a few days of stabilization while the parents decided what their course of action would be. Reviewer Y probed further and questioned whether this patient required an alternate living arrangement outside of the home. In addition, Reviewer Y questioned whether or not any family therapy had been implemented. Provider X insisted that the patient would return home within a few days, but both the parents and the patient needed time to sort things out. As far as family therapy was concerned, the provider reported that the family had pursued it for several months a few years ago, but currently they were not involved in any treatment. Further, he insisted that the problem stemmed from the patient's drug use and the provider was not able to identify any family conflict at the time of the review.

Reviewer Y notified Provider X that the acute inpatient level of care for the adolescent did not meet criteria as evidence of imminent risk was not present. The reviewer agreed that the patient evidenced patterns of impulsive, self-destructive behaviors; however, he suggested a medication and a chemical dependency assessment for the patient as well as the initiation of intensive family therapy. In terms of the immediate crisis, the reviewer suggested that the family contact other relatives to determine whether the patient could stay with one of them overnight until family therapy linkage could be initiated. As an alternative option, the reviewer suggested a 23-hour hold for the patient to ensure that the patient had been observed and assessed as not in need of acute inpatient hospitalization.

Provider X argued with the reviewer, denouncing the medical necessity criteria being used, as well as the managed care process. He notified the reviewer that he would not be held responsible for what happened to the patient on discharge, and he also insisted that he did not have time for placement issues.

Reviewer Y interjected that although he realized the provider was quite concerned about the patient as well as the patient's family, admission of this patient to such a highly restrictive, acute setting would not appropriately serve the patient's treatment needs. Although the provider and the patient's parents might be able to rest easy for a night, the patient would inevitably be discharged back to the same situation very shortly.

Provider X refused to consider alternatives suggested by the reviewer. The reviewer again notified Provider X that the current level of care was clinically inappropriate to the patient's treatment needs and level of risk. The reviewer notified the provider that unless the patient's risk status changed, the inpatient level of care would, in all likelihood, be noncertified. Subsequently the case was sent for another level of review. Prior to concluding the discussion, the reviewer gave the provider the names of custodial settings in addition to family therapists.

This example is very typical and aptly illustrates the difficulty encountered by parents, providers and reviewers with adolescent patients who are essentially conduct-disordered. As such, there is no easy solution. On the one hand, containing a very problematic adolescent on an inpatient unit may seem like a good idea to both parents and providers; however, it is medically unnecessary treatment and solves none of the real problems. In this case, an overnight stay at a relative's or at a friend's home and the initiation of intensive family therapy as well as a medication evaluation and a chemical dependency assessment might have been more appropriate than containment overnight on a psychiatric unit.

## Summary of Example #3

### Imminent Risk Criteria for Inpatient Acute Psychiatric Admission: NOT MET

♦ Although the patient was highly impulsive and evidenced a pattern of self-destructive behaviors, he was not imminently at risk for self-harm or harm to others.

### Identified Precipitant or Trigger

♦ The patient had a fight with his parents over the use of the car and threatened to run away.

### Identified Meaning of the Precipitant (Speculative)

♦ This key factor is crucial to the treatment plan for this patient. It is highly probable that the patient repeatedly had fights with his parents, during which times he also threatened to run away. Critical is the intensity of the event at this point in time. One could speculate that the parents felt helpless to control the patient any longer and sought outside intervention or containment as a last resort. Possibly, the parents realized that their son could no longer live safely at home. Again, one can only speculate on this critical issue and its real meaning to the parents as well as to the patient because the provider did not probe this concept.

### Obstacles to Wellness (Speculative)

+ Again, the reviewer can only speculate on the factors contributing to this patient's treatment issues. Family and school conflict are probable. Legal problems and substance abuse problems, as well as impulsive, self-destructive behaviors, would also appear probable. The issue of whether or not the patient can safely live in his home environment would require careful consideration. The possibility of a depressive condition would also merit review by the provider.

### Treatment Plan: (Speculative)

+ Rule out depression; assess extent of substance abuse and refer to Twelve Step Program for adolescents.
+ Determine whether custodial placement needs to be considered. Can the patient and the parents safely coexist in the home environment?
+ Psychosocial intervention—family therapy and individual therapy to help the patient and his family cope with and modify the patient's impulsive self-destructive behaviors.
+ Consider the involvement of school personnel as part of the treatment process of limit-setting and determining consequences to behaviors.

### Discharge Plan

+ As the inpatient acute level of care did not meet medical necessity criteria, given this patient's presentation, both the treatment and the discharge planning would refer to the patient's admission to a less intense, less acute level of care. Although the treatment plan is by no means exhaustive, the major interventions noted would also apply to discharge and aftercare planning.

## Example #4

A provider calls the MCO reviewer to request certification for an inpatient psychiatric admission for his 54-year-old female patient who has been diagnosed with major depression and who appears to be deteriorating rapidly. The patient has a history of treatment for depression and her family history indicates probable genetic loading on both parents' sides. The patient's mother had been treated for depression and her mother's sister had been institutionalized as a result of a major affective disorder. Her father had no known history of psychiatric treatment: however, her father's two brothers had both been alcoholics. The provider informed the reviewer that the patient appeared to be medication-resistant and he wanted to start a series of electroconvulsive shock treatments (ECT) on an inpatient basis. The patient had been complaining that her medications were not working and she indicated and verbalized to her provider that she no longer wanted to live if she felt this way—"so sick." The patient had been in outpatient therapy with medication management for several months with the same provider and had numerous outpatient treatments prior to the most recent episode. The provider reviewed the various medications he had tried with the patient to no avail. The provider had even received a consult from an expert on medications. The provider was convinced that the patient was suffering from an endogenous or biological depression and he had gained her consent for ECT. The patient had previously had ECT years earlier, which proved to be successful.

The reviewer proceeded to assess the risk of the patient in terms of suicidality, homicidality, and the presence of psychosis so severe as to render the patient unable to perform life-sustaining activities (e.g., eating, bathing, etc.). The provider reported that there was no imminent risk, but unless treated quickly, the risk for suicide might well present itself. The reviewer ruled out any medical complications that might preclude ECT. According to the provider, the patient had a supportive environment, including her husband and adult children. However, she frequently reported that she had no reason to live because she felt "so bad" most of the time. She was barely able to hold on to her part-time job at a bank. She slept approximately four hours a night and has complained of appetite problems. Recently her husband suggested they postpone their family vacation with her adult children and grandchildren until she was more herself.

The reviewer agreed that the patient might benefit from ECT. However, the reviewer questioned the necessity of an inpatient admission on an acute unit to accomplish this treatment. The provider responded that he did not feel comfortable doing ECT on an outpatient basis because the patient might experience post–ECT confusion, particularly in the beginning. The provider expressed his concerns over her ability to get to and from the hospital for treatment.

In view of the provider's concerns for the patient's safety, yet cognizant of the fact that the patient presented with no imminent risk and had no medical problems that might complicate treatment, the reviewer recommended outpatient ECT with the assistance of a VNA and transportation, as needed. This would help to ensure the patient's safety and well-being while undergoing this treatment.

Although not convinced, the provider agreed to try ECT on an outpatient basis with the agreement that the reviewer would clinically certify the VNA as medically necessary. Additionally, the reviewer reassured the provider that should the treatments result in significantly adverse effects on the patient that could not be controlled through VNA intervention, the inpatient request would be reconsidered.

This example is a very common scenario and should be evaluated on a case-by-case basis. Outpatient ECT needs to be considered prior to recommending inpatient ECT in the absence of any imminent risk or medical complications. However, cases do arise in which medical complications or severe post–ECT confusion necessitate inpatient treatment and monitoring. Oftentimes, providers are uncomfortable in performing outpatient ECT or are simply unaware of their access to outpatient ECT. The provision of ancillary support services such as home health care, for example, can make outpatient ECT more feasible. Once again, behavioral managed care attempts to provide only medically necessary treatment in the least restrictive and least intrusive environment.

### Summary of Example #4

This case is treated as an outpatient case where medical necessity criteria for outpatient treatment are applied.

### Imminent Risk Criteria for Inpatient Acute Psychiatric Admission: NOT MET

- The patient was not actively suicidal with a plan, and no medical problems were indicated to preclude outpatient ECT.

### Identified Precipitant or Trigger

- The provider's most recent session with the patient revealed that the patient was not responding therapeutically to antidepressant medications. The patient verbalized that the medications were not working and that she no longer wanted to live if she felt this sick. Her sickness made her a burden to her family such that they could not even go on their family vacation.

### Identified Meaning of the Precipitant

- Again, the crucial determinant of the course and type of treatment involves a clear identification of the meaning of a particular event for a particular patient. In this case, it can be surmised that the patient's failure to feel better after taking medications represented her inability to ever be well or normal. Her perception of always feeling sick or bad was intolerable to her, and she perceived herself as always being a burden to her family. The probability of self-harm through commission or through omission was increasing.

### Obstacles to Wellness

- This patient's biological depression is medication-resistant to a large extent. Inability to alter her feeling states so she could feel better and not always be sick.
- Patient's perception that she was a burden to her husband and to her adult children and, implicitly, that they would be better off without her.

### Treatment Plan

- Biophysiological intervention—a series of outpatient ECT treatments.
- Psychosocial intervention—VNA to ensure patient's safety and well-being while undergoing treatment; individual and family treatment to help patient cope with her perceptions about her illness and to educate her husband

and adult children on the nature and course of her illness; individual and family therapy to help the patient cope with her beliefs about being a burden to others and to help her family cope with these beliefs.

### Discharge Plan

♦ In this case, the treatment and discharge plan are relatively the same since it is probable that the patient will require maintenance ECT over time. Continued individual and family therapy will serve to foster this patient's understanding, as well as her family's understanding of her illness as well as foster more effective coping strategies for the patient herself. Another recommendation might involve linkage of the patient to a community support group dealing with depression.

## Example #5

A 55-year-old male has just been brought to the ER of a local hospital for admission to the detoxification unit. His wife had called the paramedics after her husband had become semiconscious. Reportedly, the man had a 35-year history of drinking for which he had never sought treatment. He had no prior attempts at sobriety. His heavy drinking had continued to be problematic in the marriage. The patient had been driven home from work by a colleague after "tying one on" at the local bar. According to his wife, his usual pattern involved having three to four drinks with work buddies before coming home. However, she had noticed that he was staying out longer and had started drinking earlier in the day, particularly on weekends, for the past few weeks. That same morning, the patient had called his wife to tell her that his company had finalized the decision about a merger and his job as one of the vice presidents in the company would be eliminated within three months. He and his wife had discussed this probability several months ago when he, along with other company employees, was notified about the merger. However, the patient's wife had thought that her husband had accepted the probability of a job loss, because he had actively been pursuing opening his own business prior to this announcement. According to his wife, the patient had hypertension and was on medication.

Emergency room staff noted that his blood pressure and pulse were elevated. His breathing was erratic, his face was flushed, and he was relatively incoherent. As this patient, by history, had never experienced sobriety and thus had not evidenced significant withdrawal symptoms, there was no history of seizures or delirium tremens (DTs).

The attending psychiatrist at the hospital called the MCO reviewer to request a 24-to-48-hour detox admission to monitor this patient for withdrawal. The provider indicated that the patient would be placed on a valium protocol and would be closely monitored for signs of withdrawal.

The MCO reviewer and the provider agreed that due to the patient's elevated vitals in addition to the fact that he had never withdrawn from alcohol and might evidence significant symptoms, an inpatient detox was clinically merited for at least 24 hours. The reviewer questioned the provider as to the discharge and aftercare plan as well as to the immediate problems requiring treatment. The provider reported that he had hoped to safely medically detox the patient, at which point he would attempt to get a better picture of the patient's problems and course of treatment. The reviewer suggested that the provider attempt to get further information from the patient's wife as to events preceding the admission.

### Concurrent Review—48 Hours Later
The provider notified the reviewer that the patient was medically cleared with the exception of slightly elevated blood pressure, that would soon be stabilized with continued medication. After speaking to the patient, the provider explained that the actual loss of his job was emotionally traumatizing to the patient for significant historical reasons. The patient equated the loss of his job with the failure of himself as a person and as a husband. He perceived abandonment by his family, his wife, and his friends as inevitable. He readily revealed that his own father had lost his job of 35 years at age 55 and had virtually drunk himself to death, losing his wife and his family in the process. Although he loved his father, he could not forgive him for leaving the family. The reviewer and provider discussed aftercare treatment and it was agreed that intensive marital therapy, individual treatment, as well as linkage to Alcoholics Anonymous

(AA) would be the appropriate course of action on medical clearance and discharge from the hospital.

### Summary of Example #5

#### Imminent Risk Criteria for Acute Inpatient Detox Admission: MET

- The patient evidenced elevated blood pressure and pulse rate and had a history of hypertension. Significant withdrawal symptoms were a possibility in view of his lack of any prior periods of sobriety.

#### Identified Precipitant or Trigger

- The patient had been informed that day that his job would be eliminated due to a merger.

#### Identified Meaning of the Precipitant

- The patient's father had lost his job at the same age of 55 and subsequently lost his wife and family and drank himself to death. The patient feared that his own job loss at the same age meant the same thing: essentially the loss of everyone and everything he cared about—being abandoned by everybody.

#### Obstacles to Wellness

- Need for safe medical detox and stabilization of vitals (particularly monitoring of blood pressure).
- Physiological and psychological dependence on alcohol.
- Possibility of significant withdrawal symptoms (e.g., seizures).
- Patient equated loss of his job with abandonment by others (his family, his wife).
- Unresolved grief and anger over the loss of his father and the circumstances surrounding this loss.

#### Treatment Plan

- Biological intervention—medical detox with valium protocol; 24-hour monitoring for signs of severe withdrawal and monitoring elevation of vital signs, particularly blood pressure.

- Assessment of depression and the need for medication.
- Psychosocial intervention—social detox with linkage to AA and a linkage to individual and marital therapy.

**Discharge Plan**

- Medication for depression as needed.
- Linkage to AA.
- Marital and individual treatment to help the patient cope with the loss of his job and to help the patient reevaluate his perceptions about himself and his fear of abandonment by significant others in his life. Help his family and his wife cope effectively with the patient's chemical dependency as well as with the patient's fear of loss.
- Help the patient deal with the grief about his own father as it related to his current circumstances and beliefs about himself and his family.

These cases are typical examples of provider–reviewer interactions regarding requests for inpatient care. As will be noted, however, in the next chapter, not all cases are as clear-cut in terms of the certification or noncertification of care as medically necessary. Both MCO reviewers and providers often struggle to define risk level, to identify a trigger, and to determine what type of treatment is truly medically necessary for a specific patient.

Some effective clinical reviews involve a substantial understanding of complex and interrelated cause and effect concepts in addition to the translation of these concepts into workable, achievable outcomes. The reviewer as well as the provider is constantly involved in the active clarification and redefinition of patient problems and goals. Successful clinical review from the perspective of quality patient care necessarily requires an understanding of the common pitfalls often confronting both the reviewer and the provider. The lack of clarity or definition of both a patient's reason for needing treatment and the problem that requires intervention means a corresponding lack of observability and measurability of the outcomes or results of treatment. As such, poor communication and insufficient focus are generally the greatest obstacles facing providers and reviewers.

Clear problem definition and corresponding treatment and aftercare planning enhance the degree of patient care accountability on the part of the primary provider of care in particular. Behavioral managed care has tended to increase provider responsibility toward better quality of patient care.

The following commonly encountered statements and concepts in the reviewer–provider interaction serve to illustrate some of the obstacles to clinical clarity and objectivity in the review process:

1. The patient has suicidal thoughts.
2. The patient cannot take care of himself or herself; cannot perform activities of daily living (ADLs).
3. The patient has medical problems.
4. The patient needs support from family.
5. The patient requires education about chemical dependency.
6. The patient is noncompliant with medication.
7. The patient is noncompliant with treatment.
8. The patient is not motivated.
9. The patient is not eating.
10. The patient is not sleeping.
11. The patient requires the structure of a PHP or of an IOP.
12. The patient requires stabilization.
13. The patient is psychotic, delusional, hallucinating.
14. The patient is depressed.
15. The patient is paranoid.

Of course, the list could become quite lengthy. In each case, a clear operational or behavioral translation of the concept would inevitably make the review process more effective. Many of these examples will be reviewed in the next section as well as their corresponding operational translations.

# 6

# CASE MANAGEMENT OF MENTAL HEALTH AND CHEMICAL DEPENDENCY

## *Clarification and Behavioral Definition in MCO Case Manager and Primary Provider Interactions*

### OBJECTIFYING AND TRANSLATING CLINICAL INFORMATION

As was noted in the previous chapter, one of the most significant challenges facing the MCO case manager, as well as the primary provider of care, is the translation of clinical data and concepts into objective, observable problems with workable, achievable patient outcomes. This very sophisticated and often difficult task requires both the case manager and the provider to determine precipitants and immediate triggers to the need for treatment, and to determine the specific problems or coping difficulties of the patient that the triggers or the last straw have revealed.

The following case scenarios serve to illustrate the significance of clarification and behavioral redefinition by the case manager and the primary provider.

### Case #1

**Clinical Data**

A 54-year-old man is sent to the hospital by his primary care physician (PCP) who states that the patient is not eating or sleeping and is neglecting basic ADL functions such as bathing and taking care of himself. Further, the PCP reports that the man is suicidal and requires inpatient psychiatric stabilization or acute hospitalization.

It is the job of the primary provider and the case manager jointly to redefine and to translate this information into observable and objective data to assess risk, to assess both the precipitant and the immediate trigger to this particular patient's need for treatment and to determine the medically necessary level of treatment, and after-care plan.

## Translation of Clinical Data: Examples

### Not eating means:

- The patient is 5′ 7″ and 190 pounds and can afford to skip a few meals as he has no complicating medical condition.
- The patient is 6′ 1″ and 145 pounds and has lost 15 pounds over the last three weeks due to his loss of appetite.
- The patient is not eating because he is convinced his food is poisoned.
- The patient is snacking all day and is therefore not eating regular meals.
- The patient is binging and purging and currently evidences dehydration and an electrolyte imbalance.
- The patient's weight is stable, but his appetite has decreased in the last two to three days.
- The patient is deliberately starving himself and not drinking any liquids because the patient says that he wants to kill himself.

### Not sleeping means:

- The patient usually gets seven hours of sleep per night but has been getting three to four hours in the last few nights.
- The patient sleeps most of the day and therefore is wide awake at night.
- The patient's medication is keeping the patient up at night and he appears very tired.
- The patient, who usually sleeps eight hours a night, is getting only two to three hours a night because he is evidencing manic excitement and is engaging in frenetic activity all night.

- The patient gets seven or more hours of sleep a night but wakes up three to four times a night after experiencing nightmares.
- The patient has been without any sleep for four to five consecutive nights.

**Not taking care of himself means:**

- The patient is so unaware of his surroundings and himself due to his psychiatric illness that he is unable to perform basic life-sustaining activities such as bathing, dressing appropriately for subzero weather, etc.
- The patient is becoming very forgetful and is not grooming himself as he usually does.
- The patient has a medical condition that limits his ability to move about and thus he has great difficulty performing ADLs.
- The patient sees no purpose in living and, therefore, chooses not to get up out of bed and not to take care of himself by eating, drinking, bathing, putting on appropriate clothing, etc.

**Suicidal means:**

- The patient is actively threatening to kill himself, has a plan, and has access to the means.
- The patient has fleeting thoughts of suicide approximately five minutes every day.
- The patient has obsessive thoughts about suicide but is too afraid to act on them.
- The patient will not divulge his suicide plan but has frequently talked about killing himself and has a history of near-lethal suicide attempts in the past.
- The patient is grossly out of touch with reality so as to pose a threat to himself by neglecting basic life-sustaining activities or by walking or running out into the middle of the street and being hit by a car, for example.

Though the above are just a few examples of possible translations of clinical data into behavioral, "real life" terminology, the differences in what each translation means in terms of treatment are noteworthy. For example, the two translations below mean something very different in terms of risk and the corresponding level of containment that is medically necessary for this patient. ·

## Translation #1

A 54-year-old man who is 6′ 1″ and weighs 145 pounds is sent to the hospital by his PCP, who reports that he has lost 15 pounds in three weeks and gets only two to three hours of sleep per night because he is evidencing a full-blown manic episode and is engaged in frenetic activity all night. Further, the PCP indicates that the patient is so unaware of his surroundings and his own needs that he neglects bathing and dressing, and so on. The patient is at risk for self-harm and possible death because he is grossly out of touch with reality and could feasibly run out into the street and be hit by a car, or leave the stove on, and so on.

## Translation #2

A 54-year-old man who is 5′ 7″ and weighs 190 pounds is sent to the hospital by his PCP because he has shown little interest in eating in the last few days, although his weight is stable. The patient, who usually sleeps seven hours per night, has recently been getting only about three to four hours of sleep and appears to be neglecting his basic ADLs due to forgetfulness. The patient is currently experiencing suicidal thoughts that last approximately five minutes a day, but he reports that his religious beliefs prevent him from acting on them.

Clearly, these two translations of clinical data present a patient with very different risk levels and needs for treatment. Further, these observable, objective translations give the case manager and the provider clues as to what other questions need to be asked to determine precipitants and triggers to the patient's need for treatment.

## Case #2

### Clinical Data

A 44-year-old woman is brought to the emergency room of the local hospital by her family, who have requested inpatient psychiatric admission for her. The patient is psychotic and hallucinating, according to her family. She is paranoid and a homicidal threat to her husband.

## Translation of Clinical Data: Examples

### Psychotic and hallucinating means:

+ The patient has lost contact with reality and is responding to internal stimuli or voices that are talking to her about her husband.
+ The patient has lost contact with reality and hears voices telling her to kill her husband because he is the devil.
+ The patient has periods of lucidity but at times seems to be responding to internal stimuli because she laughs and verbally responds to voices that she reports are talking to her.
+ This patient spent the last three days using cocaine and is currently experiencing visual and auditory hallucinations.

### Paranoid means:

+ The patient is hypervigilant and constantly watching over her shoulder.
+ The patient has verbalized that her husband is the devil and other people are the devil's followers who intend to harm her.
+ The patient reports that other people, including her husband, are plotting to poison her and she must protect herself from them.
+ The patient becomes very angry when criticized and believes that her husband is talking about her and making fun of her.
+ The patient hears voices telling her bad things about her husband, but they do not tell her what to do.

### Homicidal threat means:

+ The patient intends to act on the voices telling her to kill her husband by shooting him with her gun.
+ The patient loses control and throws objects at her husband when he attempts to get her to take her medication.
+ The patient often tells her husband that she feels like killing him but has never verbalized a plan.

♦ The patient is ready to physically fight with her husband whenever she perceives that he is criticizing her.

Again, these are a few examples of translations of clinical data into observable, measurable terms. They are by no means exhaustive. The meaning of the clinical data for this patient will determine the level of risk or lethality and the medically necessary level of care. Consider these two very different presentations.

**Translation #1**
A 44-year-old woman is brought to the emergency room of the local hospital by her family, who has requested inpatient psychiatric treatment for her. According to her family, the patient has lost contact with reality and is responding to internal voices that are telling her to kill her husband because he is the devil. The patient has also reported that other people are the devil's followers, who are trying to poison her, and she must protect herself. She has told her family that she will have to shoot her husband with her gun.

**Translation #2**
A 44-year-old woman is brought to the emergency room of the local hospital by her family, who has requested inpatient psychiatric treatment for her. According to the family, the patient, although lucid most of the time, currently appears to be responding to internal stimuli or voices that tell her things about her husband. The patient reports that the voices tell her bad things about him, but they do not tell her what to do. The patient is ready to physically fight with her husband whenever she perceives that he is criticizing her, and she often states that she would like to get rid of him.

## UTILIZING MANAGED CARE LANGUAGE AND CONCEPTS

Unfortunately, lack of clear communication in the MCO case manager–provider interaction often muddy the actual review process such that precipitants and immediate triggers to a patient's needing treatment as well as treatment problems and treatment interventions cannot effectively be discerned.

Consider the following clinical statements as well as their possible behavioral translations. These are among the most commonly encountered by providers and case managers and frequently perpetuate poorly defined treatment episodes. The key to making these concepts meaningful lies in the ability of both the case manager and the provider to question the what and the why for a particular patient.

    **1. The patient is noncompliant with medication.**  Although noncompliance with medication is often a key contributing factor to a patient's presentation for treatment, the significant question in defining noncompliance objectively and meaningfully is to ask why the patient in question is noncompliant. Consider the following examples to explain the why of a patient's noncompliance with medication:

- He experiences side effects that he does not like, cannot understand, or is afraid of.
- He has fleeting thoughts of suicide and feels he may overdose.
- He does not have the money to refill his prescriptions.
- He gets confused and mixes his medications.
- He believes the medications are poisoned.
- He is forgetful and this particular medication regimen requires that he remember to take medications several times a day.
- He is afraid to take medications or does not believe in taking medications due to religious beliefs.
- Other members of his household discourage him from taking his medication.
- He feels the medications are not helping him feel better.
- He is self-medicating with alcohol and other drugs and prefers these substances to the prescribed psychotropic medication.
- He is not motivated to take medication because he does not feel that he has a problem requiring medication.

    **2. The patient is noncompliant with treatment or not motivated for treatment.**  Again, although treatment noncompliance or lack of motivation are often significant contributing factors to patient recidivism to various levels of care, the key question is the why of treatment noncompliance or lack of motivation for the patient in question. Consider the following explanations or translations of the why of patient noncompliance with treatment or patient lack of motivation for treatment.

- She does not agree with or see the purpose of the treatment prescribed.
- She is very uncomfortable in groups due to her paranoia, anxiety state, etc., and wishes to pursue individual treatment instead.
- She has no transportation to the scheduled treatment.
- Her work schedule or family schedule preclude her from attending the treatment.
- She does not feel she has a problem or is in denial of her problem and refuses treatment.
- She feels she is being forced into treatment against her will.
- She is too psychologically compromised to attend treatment and requires home healthcare.
- Her therapist has become the problem.
- She is fearful she cannot afford the treatment or that her insurance will not cover the treatment.
- She is fearful that others (spouse, family, employer, etc.) will find out about her treatment.
- The patient has never been included in her treatment plan and, thus, is not aware of treatment recommendations.

**3. The patient requires stabilization.** In this case, the key question is what stabilization means for a particular patient at a particular point in time at a particular level of care. *Stabilization* can be redefined as follows:

- Medication evaluation and medication management.
- A safe medical detoxification to ensure medical stability (e.g., absence of seizures, normal vital signs).
- The absence of suicidal or homicidal intent and plan.
- The absence of psychotic features or a return to the patient's baseline level of functioning.
- The absence of, or a minimal amount of, post–ECT confusion and other side effects.

- The ability to understand his medical condition and to control it by taking medications (e.g., diabetes, hypertension).
- Control over impulsive, self-destructive behaviors (e.g., aggressive acting out, running away, truancy).
- Decreased potential for relapse through appropriate linkage to support systems and ability to cope with cravings.
- Agreement with the safety contract or no-harm contract.

Of course, the point is that stabilization, by itself, gives no information to either the provider or the case manager about the patient's specific experience of problems and specific coping difficulties. The ability to translate this concept into clear, achievable outcomes is critical.

**4. The patient requires the structure of a PHP or an IOP.** The key questions that must be asked are what would happen without the structure of the PHP or IOP, and what will the particular PHP or IOP change, reverse, or maintain. The following explanations, rightly or wrongly, are frequently among the most common justifications for these programs.

- This is the usual progression after a patient has received acute inpatient treatment.
- The patient is unsafe to himself or to others during this period of time but has the support and monitoring of family, friends, home health, and so on during the other hours of the day or night.
- The patient needs something to do or something to keep her busy during these hours because her husband is at work.
- The patient's liver or medical condition is so compromised that he requires ongoing monitoring by trained staff during this time as any relapse will result in severe medical complications, or even death.
- A PHP or an IOP is less expensive and more convenient than other types of treatment.
- The patient requires the specialized services of this particular PHP or IOP that cannot be accessed in her geographic location at a lower level of care.

- The patient is so impulsive as to require the PHP or IOP in addition to an alternate living arrangement to prevent further self-harm or harm to others, or both.
- The patient is at very high risk for complete decompensation and return to inpatient treatment due to a failed discharge and aftercare plan.
- The patient failed outpatient treatment and, thus, requires treatment in a PHP or IOP.

Unfortunately, PHPs and IOPs are frequently utilized as automatic transitions from inpatient treatment or as time fillers for patients who might be more appropriately served through focused individual or group therapy on an outpatient basis. Oftentimes, a solid link to an outpatient therapist, even on a daily basis, can meet a patient's needs far better than PHPs and IOPs. However, particularly in cases involving high risk behaviors and high potential for rapid deterioration, such programs can be very beneficial and proactive. Noteworthy is consideration by the provider, as well as by the case manager, of just how targeted and focused the PHP or IOP is. Essentially, can the PHP or IOP identify risk, patient problems, and hence gear treatment appropriately to the patient's unique needs? Alternatively, is the program simply a prepackaged series of treatment sessions that are scheduled regardless of the patient's need?

**5. The patient needs support from his family.**   The critical question is the what of support by the patient's family. *Support* may be redefined in the following terms:

- Physical support, such as in providing the patient transportation or babysitting or money to attend treatment.
- Emotional or psychological support by attending family and other group sessions.
- Understanding and accepting the symptoms and the course of the patient's illness.
- Setting firm limits with the patient.
- Letting go of the patient to enable him or her greater autonomy.
- Providing an alternate living arrangement away from the family.

♦ Encouraging the patient to take medication.
♦ Benign neglect of the patient as the treatment plan indicates.

The translations of support are numerous, as are the behavioral translations of the other clinical concepts. The next section attempts to further clarify and define the patient's problems by looking for immediate triggers to treatment episodes and to the significance of those triggers to the patient.

## IDENTIFYING TRIGGERS TO TREATMENT EPISODES

An immediate trigger to a treatment episode can be thought of as the last straw or the straw that broke the camel's back. It is perceived within the context of the patient's ongoing and multiple life experiences. The immediate trigger to treatment can be thought of as the event that touches or crosses the threshold of the particular patient's psychological, emotional, social, cultural, or biological equilibrium causing an imbalance and difficulties in coping. This imbalance, depending on its severity for the patient in question, as well as the patient's access to resources, determines the unique need of the patient for treatment intervention. The trigger may be very subtle in the context of the patient's experience; however, what the trigger represents to the patient is enough to precipitate, in some cases, a crisis and in other cases, the need for routine therapeutic intervention.                                    •

Since individuals are unique in their life experiences, as well as in their biological-physiological make ups, they also vary in terms of their internal and external sources of strength and balance, or homeostasis. Thus, the same event may be an immediate trigger to a treatment episode for one individual and not for another. For example, a husband who is sent divorce papers by his wife may experience this as an acute crisis that soon necessitates treatment, or he may experience this event as stressful but manageable within the context of his life experiences. Triggers to treatment episodes are unique to each individual, and for some patients, the immediate trigger may also be the same as the precipitant to treatment. Further, although some events almost universally trigger grief, anger, and depressive responses, such as the death of one's child or parent, whether or not such an event becomes a trigger to treatment is dependent on the individual's unique perceptions of the event and the individual's unique system for maintaining balance or equilibrium, or lack thereof.

Prior to discussing actual case scenarios, the following points are noteworthy:

1. Individuals vary widely in terms of what becomes an immediate trigger to a treatment episode.

2. Individuals vary greatly in terms of what their thresholds for maintaining balance, or homeostasis, are such that crossing over or tapping this threshold through a trigger will cause an imbalance or coping difficulties.

3. Triggers can be very obvious or quite subtle.

4. Triggers are the last straw for the patient in a series of life experiences that are ongoing.

5. Triggers can be biological, psychological, social, emotional, cultural, or a combination thereof.

6. Understanding why an individual requires treatment means identifying the immediate trigger and what the trigger means to the individual within the context of that individual's range of life experiences.

7. In some cases, an immediate trigger and a precipitant are the same event.

8. The exact same event may be a trigger to treatment for one individual but not for another.

9. The accurate identification of a trigger is significant in terms of its unique meaning to the individual and thus fosters individualized problem identification and treatment planning.

10. A trigger is the event that exposes an individual's vulnerability.

In the following two examples, the reader will review questions, events, and information relevant to the identification of triggers to treatment episodes.

In each case, we will examine the individual's ongoing life experiences and the precipitants that have culminated in the last straw event or situation that is the immediate trigger to treatment. We will also review possible methods for restoring and modifying an individual's balance or ability to cope, that will, ultimately, decrease the individual's degree of vulnerability to future occurrences.

### Case #1

A 59-year-old woman is admitted to an inpatient psychiatric unit after police discovered her on the roof of a 10-story building. According to neighbors, the patient lived alone and had been seen walking on the roof on a few occasions in the preceding two weeks. On this occasion, however, the patient appeared to be dangerously close to the edge of the roof. On admission, the patient admitted that she had planned to kill herself by jumping off the roof. When questioned further, however, the patient could not elaborate on the reasons for wanting to kill herself, except to state that she had felt the same way every August and could not stand the stress any longer. The patient's history was extensive for the treatment of depression from an early age. She had been on multiple antidepressants and had also received ECT.

### Questions

What is the immediate trigger to treatment? What does it mean to the patient in view of her life experiences? What was the precipitant culminating in the trigger to this treatment episode?

After much discussion and probing of the patient and her history, the provider has determined the following:

1. The patient appears to have a biological or endogenous depression that is largely medication-resistant but responsive to ECT treatment.

2. The patient has been employed as a school guard in a large inner city public school and is due to start back to work next month.

3. The patient lives alone, is very isolative, has little outside support and generally does not follow up with treatment linkage or treatment recommendations because she feels helpless about her depression.

**4.** The patient has, however, been in treatment over many years with a particular female therapist whom the patient relies on for support.

The provider concludes that the patient's biological depression was not treated aggressively enough. According the provider, the untreated or inappropriately treated endogenous depression is the precipitant to treatment, while the immediate trigger is the stress from the upcoming school year and the patient's return to her job as a school guard.

The reviewer is not convinced as the patient has experienced depression and has had to return to her job year after year; however, the patient has not attempted suicide or required inpatient admission for many years. The reviewer feels that something different occurred this time to necessitate crisis intervention. The reviewer suggests that the primary provider, after getting the patient's consent, discuss the case with the patient's therapist. The provider subsequently reports that the therapist has seen the patient on and off for 10 years and is, apparently, a major support for the patient. The significant point, however, is that the therapist is leaving on a business trip in a few days and will be gone for at least one to one and a half weeks. The patient was informed of this fact approximately two and a half weeks prior to this admission.

After this discussion with the patient and the patient's therapist, the following is hypothesized:

*Patient's current experience* Ongoing biological depression that is therapeutically responsive to ECT; ongoing isolation and lack of support.

*Precipitant* Return to a highly stressful job in a relatively dangerous location with little or no reinforcement.

*Immediate trigger* Therapist is leaving for a business trip and will be gone for almost a week and a half.

Once these factors have been identified, the critical question centers on the meaning or significance of this final straw or trigger to the patient causing the patient to lose balance. What, in essence, has been revealed or uncovered or tapped that has currently resulted in this patient's destabilization or inability to cope?

For the purposes of this example, the immediate trigger—the therapist leaving for a trip—represented abandonment, rejection, and loss of support and reinforcement to this patient. The ongoing experience of feelings of worthlessness, helplessness, and isolation, culminating in the final blow or trigger, crossed this patient's threshold for maintaining balance. Although the event itself might not have triggered the need for acute intervention, in this case and under these circumstances, the last straw reinforced for the patient her feelings of worthlessness and helplessness and her fear of abandonment by others. One can speculate that the patient's perceptions of being unlovable were, in her mind, confirmed and justified by the therapist's leaving.

Given this interpretation, the provider and the reviewer must now determine what problems need to be treated or what impairments require intervention to return this patient to a prior level of balance and autonomy. The following potential problems and corresponding interventions were determined from the identification of key events in this patient's immediate experience.

### Sample Treatment Plan

| Problem | Treatment |
| --- | --- |
| 1. Biological Depression | Inpatient ECT until patient is safe (i.e., not suicidal with intent, plan, or means, and will contract for safety) and then outpatient ECT as needed. |
| 2. Patient sees herself as unlovable, worthless, and deserving of rejection and abandonment by others. | Individual therapy to help patient cope with the course of her biological depression in addition to individual and group therapy to assist patient in understanding and dealing with her unrealistic beliefs about herself. |
| 3. Patient is socially isolated from others and has few friends; her beliefs and depression worsen over time with self-isolation. | Recommend a home health evaluation to determine the patient's need for an in-home healthcare staff as well as to assist the patient in attending individual and group treatment. Linkage to community self-help groups. |

Although the concepts proposed in this example are by no means exhaustive, they illustrate the real need to question the relationship of events and their unique meanings to a particular patient. The immediate trigger to treatment is highly significant in that it brings to the fore the ongoing fears, concerns, feelings, and problems experienced by the patient. Identification of the immediate trigger for a patient determines what requires treatment and what types of treatment interventions are needed.

## Case #2

A 47-year-old male is brought to the emergency room for alcohol detoxification after his wife found him in a very intoxicated condition when she returned from work. Although he has no known medical condition, his blood pressure and pulse are elevated and the primary provider plans to monitor him until his vital signs return to within normal limits. The provider is also monitoring him for any signs of seizure activity. According to his wife, the patient has a history of alcohol abuse and dependence and has never been sober for more than a few days at a time. He has had several inpatient admissions for detoxification over a 15-year period of time as he often drinks to the point of intoxification. Although he has been referred for outpatient chemical dependency treatment after his detox admissions, the patient's pattern has been to go to a few sessions of treatment and then to drop out. The patient's wife has attended a few marital sessions with her husband; however, he has also dropped out of these sessions.

A day later, the patient is clearer and medically more stable. The provider confronts the patient about his alcohol usage and about his need for treatment. The patient minimizes his usage and reports that he was overwhelmed by the performance evaluation he had received the same afternoon of his admission. The patient indicated that this event had set him back and he had simply slipped but was, overall, in control of his drinking. The patient also indicated that he had significant marital problems and suspected his wife of having had an affair about 10 months earlier. Currently, the patient and his wife were in the process of filing for divorce. In response to the provider's questions about his substance abuse treatment, the patient stated that he could stop drinking at any time and really was not very interested in treatment because he didn't think he needed it.

The critical issue in this case is identification of the immediate trigger to this patient's need for treatment and the identification of the meaning of this event. By identifying the immediate trigger within the context of this patient's experiences and within the context of the precipitant, the provider and the reviewer can determine what patient impairments require intervention and how these problems can be treated.

The patient's wife, on questioning by the attending provider, is able to provide further insight. She reports that her marital conflicts have been ongoing for years and that she and her husband had agreed to proceed with the divorce about one year ago. Although they live in the same house, for all intents and purposes, the couple is otherwise separated. The patient's wife reported ongoing financial and job problems for at least 10 years due in part to her husband's alcohol usage. The patient's wife confirmed that the recent performance evaluation at work had been disappointing and very stressful for her husband, and she anticipated that he would soon lose his job due to his alcohol usage.

Given the information provided, the provider and the case manager hypothesize the following:

*Patient's current experience*  Ongoing physiological addiction to alcohol, alcohol dependency; ongoing marital and financial problems; ongoing work performance problems; very limited periods of sobriety; and denial of problems with little follow-up on any outpatient treatment; ongoing craving for alcohol.

*Precipitant*  Recent poor job performance evaluation with probable job loss.

*Immediate trigger*  This is a case where the precipitant and the immediate trigger are really the same event. The poor performance evaluation triggered usage to the point of necessitating detox treatment.

In this case, the patient's ongoing vulnerability in terms of the physiological addiction and the cravings for alcohol may have set the stage for usage after receiving the poor job evaluation. Given this interpretation, the provider and the case manager must determine what patient problems require intervention, as well as the corresponding treatment interventions.

---

### Sample Treatment Plan

| Problem | Treatment |
|---|---|
| 1. Physiological addiction to alcohol with currently elevated vitals due to intoxication. | Safe medical detoxification to ensure normal vital signs and the absence of seizures, etc. |
| 2. Patient does not feel that he has a problem with alcohol and feels he is in control (patient is not motivated for treatment). | With the patient's consent, involve his wife and/or family in determining limits and results of his usage. With the patient's consent, involve the patient's employer in setting performance limits, performance expectations, and performance consequences. Link the patient to AA (motivate patient). |
| 3. Patient cannot handle or does not know how to handle alcohol cravings and other symptoms of physiological addiction. | Recommend individual treatment and community support groups to assist the patient in identifying symptoms of withdrawal and how to handle them. |

---

Although this is only one interpretation of Case #2, it illustrates the point that sometimes an immediate trigger can be the same as the precipitant to treatment. Although there were undoubtedly factors related to psychological addiction, this example did not focus on these factors. Significant is the possibility this patient will not, at this time, benefit from treatment other than from detoxification services. He does not appear to be motivated and he does not appear to perceive the significance of the consequences of his behavior. Because the patient feels he does not have any problem with alcohol, it is likely that he will relapse quickly and again require treatment.

In the next section, a few sample case scenarios involving lower levels of care will be reviewed in light of the factors discussed. In particular, specific outpatient cases will be examined for relevant patient experiences, precipitants, immediate triggers to treatment, and patient expectations. A PHP/IOP case will be discussed for the purposes of clarification of concepts.

These sample cases will be reviewed in relationship to two particularly unique populations—that of older adults, specifically the geriatric population, and that of adolescents. Review of these cases often involves the creative use of available therapeutic resources in addition to an understanding and working knowledge of the unique problems encountered by these populations.

# 7

# PRACTICAL CONCERNS: CLAIMS ISSUES AND THE MCO CASE MANAGER

## CLAIMS ISSUES: WHERE IS MY MONEY?

This book would not be complete without addressing the issue of claims and member and provider payment. As one of the most frequent complaints leveled by providers and members about MCOs has to do with reimbursement, I offer a few suggestions to diminish claims problems and to expedite payment. Of course, given the increasingly sophisticated computer programs, newer computer systems, and the increasing numbers of individuals who are affected by behavioral managed care, the system of reimbursement for services will likely always be somewhat problematic. However, many of the larger behavioral MCOs who clinically and financially manage mental health and chemical dependency benefits are becoming more sensitive to the need for accurate and timely payment if they are to keep their members satisfied and their providers working within their networks. The increased awareness of claims problems has propelled many revisions in existing payment systems. Primarily, the result has been an attempt to transfer paper material or hard copy information to computer databases. Although one would think that electronic systems would generate more accurate outcomes in comparison to hard copy claims data, often more individual complications have ensued. On the upside, when accurate, such systems effectively generate payment for multiple types of mental health and chemical dependency provider treatment for the millions of lives covered by the particular MCO contract.

Often problems in reimbursing providers may result in adverse effects for the patient, the provider, and the MCO. In fact, because payment for services rendered or lack of such payment or delayed or incorrect payment affects provider livelihoods, problems with reimbursement are one of the leading causes of provider resignation from a network. Such problems also result in numerous subscriber complaints and a hefty expenditure of time by MCOs. Therefore, it is important that the MCO, the provider, and the patient or the subscriber be as clear as possible in the communication of specific contract benefits and exclusions and actual treatment being delivered, and in the accurate translation of verbal or paper information into computer systems. In many cases, the correction of claims problems may simply involve a computer adjustment; however, the time spent in the reprocessing of claims and hence in waiting for payment is substantially prolonged. Of course, as no one party can control the entire system from beginning to end, the importance of clear and accurate communication and understanding up front may alleviate some of these unnecessary delays in reimbursement. Additionally, from an MCO staff perspective, the greater the number of different contracts and the greater the number of different computer programs, the greater the likelihood of errors in data translation. Unfortunately, many providers and consumers perceive the claims department of the behavioral MCO as the culprit when it comes to problematic reimbursement issues. This may be only one part of the real problem because the translation of individual patient treatment data and provider services is done more frequently by on-site staff, including MCO clinicians themselves. Further, as providers are often contracted with several MCO networks at any given time, much provider confusion exists over rates of reimbursement and types of services that are reimbursable from one MCO to another and from one benefit contract to another. Lastly, patients and/or subscribers themselves are frequently unfamiliar with their own behavioral healthcare coverage. They may switch plans and assume that benefits remain the same. Consumers are also often unaware of benefit exclusions and rely on either the provider or the MCO to educate them on how to handle the financial aspects connected to their treatment.

In sum, claims problems or reimbursement problems have no one source. Thus it is in the best interest of the patient, the MCO, and the provider to clarify as much as possible about the claims submission and reimbursement processes.

Having functioned as both a primary provider as well as an MCO case manager, I offer the following frequently occurring reimbursement problems as well as suggestions for avoiding or correcting them to both consumers and providers. Although many of the following questions are more provider-specific, the questions give the reader a flavor of common claims problems overall.

## Common Reimbursement Problems and Solutions

### Contract-Specific Rates of Reimbursement (Consumer-Specific)

Familiarity with the varying rates of reimbursement provided by a contract benefit enables the consumer to get a handle on just how much out-of-pocket expense will be billed. Some benefit structures vary considerably in rates of reimbursement for different types of treatment services. When in doubt, clarify answers to questions with the MCO. As has been previously noted, utilizing participating providers is, overall, less costly than choosing a provider who is not participating in the MCO network. The financial incentive for choosing network providers enables MCOs to maintain better clinical, administrative, and financial control over their management of a particular contract. As a consumer, consider asking the following questions in order to ensure familiarity with your behavioral health-care benefit.

**Question #1**

What is the rate of reimbursement for utilizing a participating versus a nonparticipating provider?

**Sample Response**

If you are covered by Contract X, your benefit allows you 60 percent coverage or reimbursement if you choose a nonparticipating provider and 100 percent if you choose a participating provider. If you are covered by Contract Y, your benefit will cover 50 percent if you choose a nonparticipating provider and 80 percent if you use a participating provider. You will be responsible for paying the remaining 50 percent or 20 percent, respectively.

## Question #2

My benefit covers 80 percent of my therapy charges if I use a par provider. Eighty percent of what? What do providers charge as a rate?

### Sample Response

Depending on the specific provider as well as on the particular contract and MCO, you may be responsible for a co-payment based on a preset MCO–provider contracted rate, a negotiated rate, or rate based on usual and customary fees. For the purposes of illustration, let's assume that your therapy benefit covers 80 percent of network rates. It covers 50 percent if you use a nonpar provider. For example, if you are seeking individual therapy with a licensed social worker and the social worker is an MCO-contracted provider whose preset contracted rate is $65 per 45–50 minute session, you will be responsible for the balance after 80 percent of $65 is paid. Namely, the benefit will cover $52 and your co-payment will be $13, or 20 percent of the contracted rate. If the rate for services is negotiated between the MCO and a nonparticipating provider, you may be responsible for 20 percent of the negotiated rate if given the enhanced benefit by the MCO. If the provider is a nonparticipating provider who is charging a fee based on reasonable and customary charges, that are generally higher than contracted and negotiated rates, and the provider does not want to negotiate, you will be responsible for 50 percent of that reasonable and customary rate whether it is $100 or $200. In contrast, if the MCO is able to negotiate a rate with a nonpar provider that is $80 per 45–50 minute session, for example, you would be responsible for 20 percent, or $16 out of pocket. Of course, there are multiple variations on these rates.

## Coding of Services (CPT codes) (Provider-Specific)

Another very frequent claims issue centers on confusion over CPT codes or the codes given to different types of treatment services. CPT codes are generally standardized codes but often are interpreted differently by providers and MCOs. Additionally, providers and MCOs may disagree on the types of services rendered and, hence, the codes submitted by providers on their claims will often not match up with what the MCO has entered into its data system for claims payment. This problem can be avoided by clarifying with the MCO prior to claims submission and entry the specific types of treatment rendered and the codes assigned to such treatment. Further, previously accepted codes may change, may be discarded, may require a specific sequence, or may have specific limitations depending on the computer system and program utilized by the MCO. It is important to keep current. The importance of assigning an acceptable code to a specific treatment service significantly affects the reimbursement received by a provider and by a subscriber. Denial of a claim may be due to an error in even one digit of a CPT code. The fact is that any discrepancies in MCO and in provider data will generally result in a claims denial!

Frequently both the provider and the MCO may agree that specific types of treatment are necessary; however, circumstances at the time of treatment may, necessarily, alter this. Examples would include the need for an extended therapy session, a family session rather than individual treatment, or medication in addition to a full therapy session. Such changes are part and parcel of behavioral healthcare and often simply require modification in the CPT codes by the MCO and/or the provider. These sample questions may help the reader to avoid very common reimbursement pitfalls.

### Sample Questions

1. Is there a difference between the first therapy session and remaining sessions in terms of coding?
2. Are ancillary services such as home healthcare coded differently?
3. Is the provider fee inclusive or noninclusive in the treatment program rate? Exclusions or noninclusive services generally require separate codes.
4. How do I bill for ECT in the hospital or ECT on an outpatient basis? Do I need to include a code for the anesthesiology group used?
5. How do I bill for an extended phone consult?
6. How do I bill for special services such as medication consults, psychological testing, and so on?

## Precertification Requirements and Penalties (Provider-Specific)

Currently, almost all behavioral healthcare services require some type of precertification. The exception to this is generally found in emergency situations; however, providers and patients are given a time limit in which to notify MCOs even about emergency services. Of course, individual exceptions may be made to these requirements. Generally penalties are incurred by either the provider or the member, or both, if the precertification requirement is not met. Many MCOs have designated grievance committees that oversee such issues, particularly in compelling cases. Exceptions exist where, for example, a patient's mental status is too impaired and no family contact exists to determine the patient's coverage at the time of an emergency admission. Providers in such cases may only discover the patient's coverage after stabilization or even well after discharge. These cases are, however, rare exceptions. Unfortunately, even participating providers fail to precertify with the MCO for a number of reasons. These reasons may include lack of knowledge regarding the precertification requirement by provider staff, communication failure, lack of staff after regular business hours within a provider site, or even confusion regarding precertification in different MCO systems. Oftentimes, providers believe that they have precertified by calling and giving patient demographics. This may satisfy some MCO precertification requirements but may fall short with others. Failure to precertify treatment or a request for treatment often results in a financial penalty to the provider. Unfortunately, many providers still fail to precertify treatment even on an outpatient basis and find later, to their dismay, that they simply are not reimbursed for the nonprecertified treatment sessions. In other contracts, however, allowances may be made for nonparticipating providers whose treatment sessions are not precertified. The following may be useful questions to ask to avoid the potential for nonreimbursement.

### Sample Questions

1. Does the MCO–provider contract require precertification? If so, what will satisfy this requirement? Demographics, clinical information, etc.?

2. Is there a time period for precertification? Who do I call after hours? What is the 24-hour MCO phone number?

3. What type of circumstances are considered emergency situations or exceptions?

4. Can I bill the patient or the subscriber for the financial loss incurred due to a precertification failure?

5. How do I grieve the penalty assessed to me?

6. Do the same precertification requirements apply to nonparticipating providers?

7. Do the same precertification requirements apply to different levels of care?

8. Who can precertify treatment?

9. Does precertification mean calling the MCO from the emergency unit, from a patient's home, or when the patient is first admitted to the unit?

10. Can the facility utilization review department call the MCO the following day to precertify?

11. Is a physician assessment necessary to precertify a patient admission?

## Dates of Treatment Services (Provider-Specific)

Oftentimes, problems in reimbursement of claims arise from differences in treatment dates certified in a computer system and actual dates of service. Further, lack of entry or incorrect computer entry by the MCO, for any number of reasons, will generally result in reimbursement problems. Simple examples of these circumstances include the following:

• As a provider of individual therapy, you have seen a patient almost weekly between January and March. The MCO has also certified treatment through the end of March but not beyond. You, however, have not used all the originally certified sessions and have continued to see the patient through April because it is medically necessary for the patient in question. On submitting your bill for payment to the MCO claims department, your dates of service do not correspond to the dates of service in the computer system, resulting in nonpayment of the claims or only partial payment of the claims. Because this is a very common scenario about which many MCOs are aware, a call by the provider requesting an extension of the end date of services may be all that is required. In some cases, however, adjustments, where possible, become more complicated and time-consuming.

♦ Another common example includes the situation where a provider has been given certification by the MCO verbally, but for one reason or another, that information has not been entered into the computer system or has been entered incorrectly, or only partially. Often a partial or incorrect data entry can be readily corrected. However, the absence of data entry, particularly in outpatient cases where there may be only one paper record of certification, may become problematic and may result in a request to retroactively review the case by the MCO. The provider is advised to contact the case manager and to keep careful records of any verbal or written certification.

**Sample Questions: Consider the following questions prior to submitting a claim:**

1. Do the start and end dates of service match up with what was originally certified by the MCO? If not, how do I correct this discrepancy?

2. Can end dates of service be extended by the MCO? If not, what adjustment can be made such that I will receive reimbursement for services rendered?

3. Does the MCO routinely send providers written confirmation of certification? If not, what is the procedure to establish verification of certification utilized by the particular MCO?

4. Who do I, the provider, contact at the MCO in order to correct this type of claims problem?

5. How do I bill for an emergency visit or session?

### Demographic Information on Claims (Provider-Specific)

Although errors or omissions in demographic information are simple to correct, these errors often cause significant claims delays and initial claims denials. The provider needs to ensure that all identifying information such as the correct spelling of the patient's name, the subscriber's name, the contract the individual is insured under, the date of birth, and Social Security number, and so on are correct. Frequently, the wrong family member is identified or an incorrect Social Security number is submitted, resulting in a claims delay or denial.

## Benefit Limitations, Exclusions, and Nonpayment (Provider-Specific)

At times a provider will bill for services that are not a covered benefit under a particular contract. For example, billing for residential treatment when a particular contract specifies this service as an exclusion will result in nonpayment unless the MCO has made an exception to flex the benefit and has noted this during data entry. If the provider is a residential facility that is being certified for medically necessary treatment only, billing must reflect the treatment, not room, board, and so on. Similarly, if you have been informed by the MCO that, for example, educational testing for the purposes of placement is not considered medically necessary treatment and is therefore not a covered benefit, do not expect payment from the MCO if you proceed to perform the testing and bill for it. To summarize, as a provider you must be aware of the specifics of a patient's contract. Even if you believe a specific service or treatment is covered or should be covered under a patient's insurance contract, do not assume that it is. Further, although specific services, such as growth therapy, etc. may be excluded under some contracts, check with the MCO for any exceptions. Contracts vary in terms of their benefits and exclusions.

## Medical versus Psychiatric Services (Provider-Specific)

Oftentimes behavioral MCOs will receive claims for what are considered medical services. Much confusion still exists over such differences, particularly in cases of detoxification and in cases of eating disorders. Some treatment services will include both medical and psychiatric care. The key is to determine what is covered and, hence, reimbursable by the behavioral MCO. For example, alcohol detoxification is often performed on a medical unit but billed as a psychiatric treatment and reimbursed as such. Alternatively, extensive lab work and so on may be performed while a patient is on a psychiatric unit for treatment of a life-threatening psychiatric illness; however, such services may be billed and reimbursed under the patient's medical coverage rather than under the patient's behavioral health care coverage. In other cases, however, a medical specialist such as a neurologist or an endocrinologist, may be utilized during psychiatric treatment in order to clarify diagnoses or treatment. This use of specialists is often noted in cases where a patient has a significant and severe reaction to medication, for example. These medical services may, in fact, be reimbursable under the patient's psychiatric benefit in such a case. In summary, you, as the provider, need to clarify with the MCO what services are covered by the patient's medical carrier and what services are covered under the patient's mental health and chemical dependency benefit.

### Noncertification and Nonreimbursement (Consumer- and Provider-Specific)

In those cases where treatment is not considered medically necessary by the MCO and is clinically noncertified, the provider, whether a facility or an individual, will not, generally, receive payment for such services. As either the provider or the consumer, it is important to question the MCO regarding what services and what service dates will not be covered or reimbursed. However, exceptions do exist. For example, treatment may be clinically noncertified but may be administratively certified by the MCO for any number of reasons, including the lack of alternative treatment facilities or providers necessary to meet the patient's needs. Further, treatment may be clinically noncertified at one level of review but subsequently found to meet criteria at another level of review and thus be reimbursable. The following questions may help the consumer and the provider in understanding noncertification and lack of financial reimbursement where treatment is noncertified.

#### Sample Questions

1. What are the MCO's policies and procedures regarding noncertification and levels of appeal?
2. Have I exhausted all levels of appeal?
3. What are the exact services and dates of service that are not reimbursable? Why?
4. Is the recommended alternate level or type of care available and accessible to the patient? If not, what will be clinically certified?
5. Is the level or type of care partially covered? If so, which part?
6. Are other providers and/or types of treatment services that were utilized during the noncertified treatment

covered and therefore reimbursable? If so, what providers and/or what types of treatment? For example, are the attending psychiatrist's medication follow-ups with the patient covered even though the treatment level or type of service is clinically noncertified and nonreimbursable?

7. When is treatment considered not clinically medically necessary but still reimbursable, administratively, by the MCO?

8. Is the treatment not reimbursable due to noncertification or due to nonprecertification? The reader needs to understand the differences in status since MCOs utilize different protocols and procedures in each case. Nonprecertification involves administrative requirements, and noncertification generally involves the application of clinical criteria.

## Clinically Certified Treatment Which Is Nonreimbursable (Consumer- and Provider-Specific)

Although this situation is the exception, it still occurs and the provider is advised to routinely verify a patient's benefit status, where possible, prior to treatment. In some cases, a patient's treatment may be clinically certified but not financially reimbursable due to the patient's benefit status. This status may include the patient's ineligibility for coverage, the patient's exhaustion of benefit status or the lack of any information about a particular patient's benefit status. Generally, the MCO will have determined the patient's status prior to a treatment referral; however, disclaimers are routinely conveyed to providers and to patients or subscribers in the event that a patient's status precludes reimbursement. Although a provider cannot control all possible factors contributing to ineligibility, the provider can take some precautions. For example, know a patient's benefit limitations. If the patient is allotted a specific number of covered chemical dependency treatments per lifetime, or a certain number of outpatient sessions per year, keep an accurate record of session numbers and dates such that you are aware of potential benefit exhaustion. Routinely question the case manager about allowances for specific treatments on a yearly basis as well as in terms of lifetime limits. Be aware of the beginning and ending dates for different contracts covering different patients. As has been noted previously, not all contracts are based on the calendar year. Further, some benefits have strictly monitored lifetime maximums for specific types of treatment, after which the patient must self-pay for any further such treatment. The consumer is similarly advised to be knowledgeable about benefit limitations. When in doubt, the consumer is advised to access the member services division of the payer or to access the customer service department of the behavioral MCO for information.

### Claims Submission (Provider-Specific)
Simply put, make sure the right claim is sent to the right place. Although the reader may well be surprised at the simplicity and obvious nature of this statement, the fact is that oftentimes clerical errors such as mailing the wrong form to the right place or mailing the right form to the wrong place will undoubtedly delay claims processing. It is important to determine what claims form is utilized by the specific MCO. Further, determine whether claims for services at the enhanced rate or at the in-network rate are mailed to the same address as claims submitted for out-of-network services, that carry with them a reduced benefit. Depending on the particular contract, there may be a difference for claims submissions. Although providers may submit claims information on their own letterhead, it is more expeditious to submit standardized claims forms. Provider letterhead claims documentation often lacks necessary information for payment purposes or may be denied because the information contained is too time-consuming for a claims department to process.

### Miscellaneous Items and Nonreimbursement (Provider-Specific)
It is encouraging to note that most MCOs have strong financial and administrative incentives built into their contracts to quickly and accurately pay claims to providers. In fact, MCOs may be assessed financial penalties for delays in claims processing. Further, an MCO's clinical motivation to be able to keep quality providers within its network by ensuring a quick claims turnaround represents a further incentive. However, even very minor data discrepancies between what is entered by the MCO for claims reimbursement and what the provider submits on the claims form for reimbursement can result in a denial of reimbursement altogether or errors in what

is reimbursed. Consider the following points in helping to ensure accurate and timely reimbursement.

**Points to Consider**

1. Ensure that all information, no matter how trivial it may appear, is accurately and legibly completed on the appropriate claims form. Submit it to the correct address.

2. Ensure that you contact your MCO in writing regarding any changes in address, phone number, degree, education, office locations, etc., to ensure accurate updating of the MCO's provider database.

3. Contact your MCO if you are not sure of a particular item on your claims form. This, although time-consuming, will save you in the long run. For example, discrepancies in group practice titles and tax identification numbers are commonplace. Be clear on whether you are required to bill as an individual provider with an individual tax identification number or whether you need to bill under your group practice name and group practice identification number.

4. Clarify with the MCO case manager the type of service as well as the location of the service being billed. Very frequently, simple discrepancies in individual versus group treatment or in inpatient treatment versus outpatient treatment will result in a claims denial.

5. Familiarize yourself with a patient's benefit coverage such that you will have a working knowledge of the reimbursement you can expect to receive. Also, determine beforehand what amount, if any, the patient is required to pay to you directly in the form of a co-payment.

6. Include an accurate diagnosis on your claims form.

7. Confer with the MCO on billing codes for specialized services such as home health, expert consults, transportation, telephone consults, psychological testing, and so on.

8. Although clinically, you may be justified in billing for a specific treatment, if this treatment is not entered in the MCO data system as certified, the claims will be denied or questioned.

9. You may know the difference between the intermediate levels of care such as PHP and IOP, but the claims department will not. Don't expect the claims department to figure out what you really mean. Bill using the specific code attached to the specific treatment rendered. Specifically, if you and the MCO case manager have agreed that a specific type of treatment falls within a specific treatment category, be very clear on how that item is being entered into the system by the MCO case manager to ensure that you have the same code when billing. This scenario frequently surfaces where the provider and the MCO case manager mutually agree that although a program may be included as a PHP, for example, the services rendered in terms of treatment and numbers of hours are more accurately submitted under the category of IOP. Problems in reimbursement occur where one party indicates PHP, while the other party indicates IOP. Check with your case manager when you are uncertain about how a particular service will be entered by the MCO. MCOs vary in their coding of different levels and types of care.

10. Persist! Remember, the squeaky wheel gets the oil. Claims problems are frequent but generally correctable. Many providers are routinely transferred from one department to another in an attempt to collect on a claim. You are advised to contact your case manager as to what department will handle your particular problem. Oftentimes, the case manager can correct the problem or will do the leg work for you. The case manager has a vested interest in ensuring that you get paid, particularly if you are a preferred provider. The case manager cannot write your check; however, he or she can effectively get the ball rolling.

In cases where you run into a dead end, you may want to put the issue in writing and speak to the account manager for the contract you are servicing if the case manager is unable to correct the claims problem. This is particularly true in cases involving large financial reimbursements.

Blasting the claims department will not get the problem corrected! As a provider dealing with different MCOs, you may have good, creative suggestions about correcting your claims problems. Although many claims problems are not readily apparent, you may get a clue by carefully reviewing your own records. MCO staff are more amenable to putting other issues on hold to check out your claims issue if you have some idea of what the problem is and a suggestion about how to correct it.

## GETTING THE MOST OUT OF YOUR MCO CASE MANAGER

This book would also be incomplete without suggesting a few tips for the provider and the subscriber to use in fully accessing the MCO case manager as a key resource. In fact, even die-hard opponents of managed care have been able to work more effectively with MCOs by collaborating with the case manager rather than by fighting. For the subscriber, some of these tips will, hopefully, shed some light on the process of behavioral managed care and managed care, in general. The secrecy surrounding managed care continues to have more to do with individual misinformation, poor communication, and fear than it has to do with inherent and opposing philosophies and principles of treatment. The reader may be able to work the system better by considering the following points.

For the provider, the case manager is a resource and can help make the behavioral managed care process easier. In many instances, the case manager had or currently has a private practice and has been in the position you are in currently as a primary provider. As a major problem in behavioral managed care continues to be that of ignorance and miscommunication, ask a lot of questions. Ignorance in managed care is not bliss. It means a poor working relationship with the MCO, numerous requests for noncertification, and the increased potential for nonreimbursement of services. As a provider, you might consider the following tips in working with the MCO case manager.

1. Request a copy of the MCO's guidelines and criteria for medical necessity.
2. Ask what the MCO's policy and procedures are on precertification and nonprecertification.

3. When informed that a treatment service is not medically necessary and is not being clinically certified, ask for examples of criteria being used to make the determination and ask how you can avoid this type of situation in the future.

4. Ask how the MCO determines the distinction among different levels of care, particularly between the intermediate and outpatient levels.

5. From the get-go determine whether placement services, residential services, and rehabilitation services, and so on are typically covered.

6. Behavioral managed care has its own language. Learn it! Know what is meant by a precipitating event and a trigger to treatment. Determine what the potential stressors are for your particular patient.

7. If you don't know the answer, say so! You are more likely to receive helpful information from an MCO case manager who, generally, wants to establish a good working relationship with you.

8. Establishing an adversarial relationship with the MCO case manager is a lose–lose situation. Use your clinical skills to answer the questions and to avoid powerplays. Since many MCO case managers are, themselves, still learning the ropes within the MCO system, pulling rank only serves to reinforce inadequacies and to increase defensiveness.

9. If you question the clinical soundness of advice or a decision, hold your ground. You are in a good position to discuss your concerns because you have the most direct contact with the patient. The case manager must rely on your input to make decisions.

10. When offered additional help in the form of an expert opinion or a consult, take it! Too often, providers consider such a suggestion as an indication of their own inadequacy or failure to handle a patient's treatment. Simply speaking, providing a second or even a third opinion to a provider is a lot of extra work for the case manager. Additionally, it is generally at cost to the MCO.

Given these factors, most case managers will only offer you an expert consult when you have exhausted all other treatment options and where outside intervention may help in the patient's treatment. Additionally, a second opinion helps you, the provider, by taking you off the hook in cases of particularly high-risk patients. You share the responsibility and the liability for care with another clinician.

11. Having a working relationship with the MCO case manager does not mean that you have betrayed your own principles and philosophies about mental health and chemical dependency treatment or that you have sold your soul to managed care. It simply means that for the good of the patient, as well as for the purposes of financial reimbursement, you are able to work within the current system with its management oversight. Fighting managed care is like fighting city hall. Don't waste your time! In one form or another, managed care is effecting most of us and is here to stay, it seems. Although case managers from different MCOs may use different criteria to determine certification, the message is the same. Simply, oversight and management of patient treatment helps to ensure that only medically necessary care in the least restrictive environment is provided.

12. Managed care is highly competitive and demanding. Get used to it! The pressure to effectively produce positive treatment outcomes for patients while limiting cost is very difficult and requires clinical creativity and sophistication. Not every treatment technique is effective, and not every outcome is good. MCO case managers are always searching for more creative ways to manage care that will result in effective treatment outcomes. When dealing with the case manager, offer suggestions and alternatives. Together you, the provider, and the case manager may be able to come up with even better options for patient care than either of you alone.

13. The case manager is not the enemy and noncertification or the denial of treatment is not the case manager's goal.

In reality, the opposite is true. Truly sophisticated MCO
case managers will attempt to work proactively with the
provider to avoid the situation where a patient's care is
noncertified. Used as a tool, noncertification can improve
patient care. However, using noncertification as a
weapon truly defeats the purpose of managed care by
causing unnecessary patient and provider distress. If the
provider feels that noncertification is being used for
questionable reasons, discuss this with the case manager.
The provider's input is vital to the success of the patient's
treatment.

14. Paperwork is part of the managed care system and is not
an attempt to make the process more difficult. In reality,
most case managers would opt for much less paper flow,
because it would mean less work. Until all computer
systems are perfect and until all MCOs and providers are
computer literate, paperwork, in some form or another, is
here to stay.

15. Behavioral managed care is about the best patient care.
Although the provider and the case manager may
disagree, it is important to maintain perspective during
the process. The question of what is in the best interest of
the patient is key.

16. Even case managers with years of experience may
mistake a provider's lack of knowledge for provider
resistance. Further, many case managers may feel
intimidated by a provider's approach and/or credentials
and be disinclined to educate the provider or in some
cases to get the answers needed to make an informed
decision about certification. This type of scenario serves
no one's best interest. You, as the provider, know your
own level of tolerance for the managed care process, as
well as your own limitations regarding a working
knowledge of the system. Again, ask questions,
particularly if you are stuck or don't know how
something works within the system. Resistance affects
providers in different ways, from outright lack of
cooperation with the process to the more subtle,

undermining and possible sabotaging of a patient's treatment. In one way or another, resistance surfaces. If you find that you, as a provider, simply cannot adapt to the particular MCO system, attempt to participate in another behavioral MCO network that may be a better fit.

# 8

# THE MOST FREQUENTLY ASKED QUESTIONS ABOUT BEHAVIORAL MANAGED CARE

**A**ctive involvement in and questioning of the behavioral managed care process by consumers and providers can significantly impact both the consumer's degree of satisfaction and the provider's ability to ensure quality patient care and tangible outcomes. Although the delivery of mental health and substance abuse services through behavioral managed care organizations is commonplace nationwide, consumers as well as providers are frequently reluctant to question these managed care organizations. This hesitancy appears to be, in part, due to the sense of taboo surrounding the treatment of mental illness and chemical dependency. Although consumers and providers of medical managed care also share this hesitancy, the greater degree of precision and outcome objectivity of medical science enables it to escape the shroud of secrecy and even shame that oftentimes encompasses the treatment of mental illness and chemical dependency.

Behavioral MCOs, which increasingly emphasize outcome studies, measures of consumer satisfaction, and measures of provider performance, are keenly aware of the need to dispel the myths surrounding the treatment of psychiatric problems. MCOs further realize that involved and informed consumers and providers tend to be more satisfied with the behavioral managed care organization. By encouraging consumers and providers of services to ask questions about the processes of treatment, service delivery, and administrative and financial aspects of care, MCOs improve their abilities to provide quality care while containing costs. This is particularly noteworthy during the processes of utilization review and case management where ignorance or miscommunication about expectations on the part of the provider or on the part of the case manager, or both, may have negative effects on the patient, often placing the patient in the middle of an adversarial relationship.

Many MCOs employ trained customer service representatives to clarify and to answer specific questions and complaints posed by consumers and providers. However, often the real concerns and questions of consumers and providers are either not directly asked or are not clearly or appropriately answered. This very common problem can be corrected through the greater education of both providers regarding treatment expectations and consumers regarding their own treatment.

Breaking through the secrecy and leveling the playing field, so to speak, between the consumer and the provider can only improve the MCO's ability to effectively and responsibly manage psychiatric care.

The following questions are those most commonly encountered by MCO staff in communications with consumers as well as with providers on behalf of their patients. In this section subscribers are also the consumers of treatment.

### What does my benefit plan cover for mental health and chemical dependency? What about deductibles and co-pays? What doesn't it cover?

Generally, most benefit plans provide for coverage of standard services such as a specific number of inpatient chemical dependency and/or mental health days per calendar or contract year in addition to coverage for outpatient chemical dependency and mental health treatment. Additionally, many plans cover treatment in intermediate levels of care, including PHP and IOP. However, benefits vary greatly in terms of allowances and exclusions. For example, some benefit plans include unlimited access to treatment, while others set limits on treatment sessions and treatment days. Further, some plans cover only in-network provider services, while others cover out-of-network services, generally at a lower rate. Still other plans may differentiate between mental health treatment and chemical dependency treatment and vice versa, covering acute care for one and not for the other. Physician fees may or may not be included in contracted hospital rates. If physician services are billed separately, the benefit plan will generally cover a percentage of the charges depending on the physician's status as a contracted or non-contracted provider.

Many benefit plans do not cover residential treatment or ancillary support services, such as home health care, transportation, or specialized consultations. Some benefit plans do not cover treatment where the primary diagnosis is an Axis II diagnosis, such as personality disorder, and other plans may not cover traditional V Code diagnoses, such as parent–child problems or marital conflicts. However, exceptions to every benefit package exist and in specific cases, the MCO will agree to flex an otherwise excluded benefit. In most cases, benefit plans for outpatient treatment will not cover such items as experimental vitamin therapy, growth therapy, specialized sleep disorder treatment that is experimental, or therapy for the purpose of documenting stability prior to undergoing a sex change operation.

As exceptions do exist, a consumer should read the specifics of the benefit package carefully. Because much of the reading material sent to subscribers and providers is confusing and readily open to misinterpretation, consumers and providers are urged to call the benefit hotline, if available, or the customer service department of the MCO for greater clarification. This is particularly true in cases where benefits may be quite limited and where benefits do not exist for out-of-network or out-of-state treatment.

Many plans require the subscriber to pay a deductible, or specific amount of out-of-pocket expenses, for a given calendar or contract year prior to covering any mental health or chemical dependency claims. This deductible for an individual is generally different from that for a family and varies in terms of the specifics of the healthcare plan. In some plans, the consumer may pay no deductible. In many plans, consumers are also required to pay a co-payment or a specified amount of money each time services are rendered. For example, a consumer may be required to pay a co-payment of $50 per inpatient day up to a specified maximum of $250 for that inpatient stay, from which point on the health plan may pick up 100 percent of charges. Further, outpatient visits may require a co-payment of $5, $10, $15, and so on out-of-pocket for each therapy visit.

Lastly, in many benefit packages, allowances are made in those cases where psychological evaluations for the purpose of greater diagnostic clarity and treatment clarity are required. Each benefit plan varies in terms of its flexibility and in its degree of negotiability.

### What is the difference between an in-network and an out-of-network benefit? What is the difference to me?

In some benefit plans, such as in the case of many HMOs, no benefit for using an out-of-network or noncontracted provider may be payable. In other plans, using a nonparticipating hospital or provider means that the consumer will be responsible for a greater percentage of the billed amounts. In plans having a PPO (preferred provider organization), consumers are given the option of choosing a nonparticipating provider; however, they frequently may also have a higher deductible as well as a higher co-payment. In some cases, the maximum lifetime benefit for using out-of-network providers may be substantially less than that applied when using in-network providers.

The consumer should be aware that MCOs develop and maintain networks of providers to ensure financial, clinical, and administrative control over mental health and chemical dependency treatment. The lower percentage of out-of-pocket expenses to consumers afforded by a participating provider serves as a financial incentive for the consumer to utilize the network. Further, whereas participating providers, with some exceptions, have agreed to the policies and procedures inherent in the MCO–provider contract, nonparticipating providers, with few exceptions, cannot readily be held to the same standards of quality and accountability. Also the costs of treatment with a noncontracted provider are generally not under the control of the MCO and are often much higher than contracted rates with participating providers. Some nonparticipating providers, however, will opt to participate in the utilization review and case management processes and will agree to negotiate provider rates with the MCO.

Exceptions to these generalizations exist, particularly in cases where no participating provider is available for a specific type of treatment in a specific geographic location. In such cases, the consumer may have no other option than to see a nonparticipating provider. In these instances, benefit plans generally will reimburse costs at a rate comparable to what would have been paid if the consumer had been able to utilize a participating provider or at what is known as the "enhanced rate." This is frequently noted in cases involving eating disorders and in the treatment of children and adolescents, particularly in remote geographic locations. In other instances, the behavioral MCO will pay the provider at a rate that is "usual and customary" for the service provided or, where possible, the MCO will negotiate a lower rate of reimbursement with the provider. Overall, MCO provider networks are still evolving in terms of number of providers, geographic location, and provider specialties. MCOs who are aware of their network limitations attempt to accommodate to the needs of their consumer populations.

## What is the difference to me between an HMO and a PPO?

Overall, the difference in the variations of HMO and PPO health care models involves the degree of freedom of choice a consumer can exercise. This applies to the choice of provider, with generally greater freedom of choice afforded in a PPO. PPOs also typically allow for coverage out of network; whereas HMOs cover only provider treatment that is in-network or within the HMO panel.

Noteworthy is the fact that both types of plans restrict to some degree the consumer's access to mental health and chemical dependency provider care and also restrict the provider's ability to participate in a given consumer healthcare system (Baldor 1996, 27). As a result, the POS model (Point of Service) that involves both HMO and PPO options has evolved to allow consumers greater freedom of choice. Currently, however, the expense of such a healthcare plan is higher and requires greater out-of-pocket consumer expenses in terms of deductibles and co-payments than either of the other models, generally.

Generally speaking, the consumer who opts for greater treatment, provider, and geographic choice and who is willing to pay, on average, higher monthly premiums, higher deductibles, and higher co-payments may opt for a healthcare plan having a PPO. Alternatively, the consumer who is more comfortable with treatment in a specified geographic location, with specified providers, but with generally lower out-of-pocket costs may opt to join an HMO.

## What is an MCO Provider or an MCO Provider Group?

The term *provider* for most MCOs refers to an individual or group of individuals or an institution determined as qualified to provide mental health and/or chemical dependency services by the MCO. This term may apply to a social worker, an addictions specialist, a psychiatrist, a hospital, an agency, an anesthesiology group, a home health group, an ambulance service, and so on. Providers may be found in one geographic location or may have multiple offshoots or affiliate groups located across the state or nation. The provider is most frequently a licensed or credentialed mental health and/or chemical dependency professional; however, this is not always the case. Some MCOs reimburse providers who are BA or MA level staff, either as individual providers or as providers under the umbrella of a larger licensed group, licensed professional, or licensed institution. The determination of the types and levels of providers who are reimbursable for treatment is dependent on the MCO–payer contract. Many consumers think of individual therapists as providers. The concept of a hospital or of an agency or of an ambulance service as a provider is often confusing.

Where possible, consumers are advised to opt for licensed and credentialed providers and providers such as hospitals that have achieved accreditation from outside surveying bodies. Overall, these providers, unlike noncredentialed, nonlicensed or nonaccredited providers, have had to meet at least the minimal quality of care performance standards set forth by the particular state and/or licensing, credentialing, or accrediting bodies.

Currently, MCOs, predominantly, include licensed entities or individuals within their networks, unless a particular healthcare benefit plan specifies otherwise. However, it is always important for a consumer to ask questions about the background of the provider or providers he/she is referred to for treatment. These include questions about licensing, background, areas of specialty, level of degree, and so forth. Consumer questioning will often lead to a better consumer–provider fit as well as help to dispel various myths or misinformation about different types of providers. For example, many consumers simply to do not know the difference between a psychologist and a psychiatrist. Often a consumer is unaware of the fact that psychiatrists can prescribe medication.

When unsure, consumers should ask what services they can expect to receive when referred to a provider. Many consumers are unaware, for example, that, in most states the MD (generally the psychiatrist) is responsible ultimately for their discharge from mental health and chemical dependency treatment, particularly at the higher levels of care such as inpatient treatment.

### What is precertification? Who is responsible for it and what happens if there is no precertification?

MCOs are increasingly moving towards precertification of all treatment by the participating providers, as well as by the consumers of treatment, whether that be the actual patient, spouse, or family member. There is a financial incentive attached to the precertification process such that lack of precertification by the facility or consumer, or both, may result in a financial loss to the consumer in terms of a penalty and a financial loss to the provider in terms of nonpayment for treatment sessions or days of treatment.

Traditionally, precertification simply meant calling in demographics regarding a patient such as name, address, phone number, and provider name. MCOs are moving toward precertification as meaning the conveyance of clinical information about a patient by a provider who is requesting authorization for treatment of the patient.

Precertification is generally taken to mean notification of the MCO by the consumer or the patient's family or a request for treatment or a review of clinical information by the provider of services with an MCO clinician prior to, or, in cases of emergency, at the time of the admission to treatment. Typically, MCOs are requiring precertification with clinical information from the provider for all levels of care from acute inpatient hospitalization to routine outpatient treatment.

It is critical for the consumer to understand that precertification does not guarantee coverage of treatment. First, although a provider may precertify treatment with an MCO clinician, the requested level of care may not be congruent with the particular

MCO's medical necessity criteria. Further, even if a precertification of treatment does meet medical necessity guidelines, the patient may be found to be ineligible for treatment benefits. Although MCOs generally avoid the ineligibility problems by checking the patient's benefit status, mistakes do occur. In most cases, the consumer is informed directly by mail or by phone regarding benefit ineligibility or benefit exhaustion.

Noteworthy is the fact that MCOs do not dictate treatment but rather attempt to guide, educate, and monitor providers. Hence, treatment that is noncertified due to lack of medical necessity by the MCO does not necessarily mean that a patient is not admitted to treatment or is automatically discharged from care. By the same token, nonprecertification does not mean that a patient cannot access services. A consumer may have followed necessary precertification protocols; however, the provider may not. In such a case, many MCOs, except where individual provider contracts dictate otherwise, penalize the provider and not the consumer. For most MCO providers, the necessity of clinical precertification or clinical preauthorization is part of the MCO–provider contract.

Exceptions are also made when it comes to the precertification process. For example, a specific hospital may admit a psychiatric patient who is suicidal without precertifying simply because the patient is unable to identify his or her health care plan because of diminished or compromised mental status. In such a case, depending on the specific MCO, it is likely that when the case is reviewed, neither the hospital nor the patient may be held financially accountable or responsible.

The consumer should be aware that some providers will attempt to collect on unpaid treatment revenues through balance billing. This means that a provider such as a hospital may bill the patient or consumer for any unpaid charges after the claim has been paid by the MCO. This practice is generally prohibited, except where specified in particular MCO–provider contracts. However, many consumers are often unaware of the prohibition against balance billing by most MCO–contracted providers. Additionally, consumers of treatment may, unwittingly, sign a consent at a provider facility in which they agree to pay the balance of all unpaid claims. The attempt to balance bill is frequently observed in cases where treatment is clinically noncertified and where the patient continues in treatment, or where providers attempt to make up for financial losses due to their own failures to clinically precertify with the MCO.

Consumers are encouraged to ask questions regarding their responsibility in the precertification process as well as regarding their financial liability for unpaid provider treatment services. However, it is also important to note that not all MCO–provider contracts prohibit balance billing of the patient. The consumer should be aware of those providers who have this option.

## I'm very dissatisfied with my provider. What can I do about this?

Various options exist for the consumer to file complaints and to change providers. Commonly, a call to the clinician managing your case or a call to the intake department, where one exists, will enable the consumer to flag a problematic provider or request another provider. Frequently, consumers are directed to the customer service department and the provider relations department of an MCO when a problematic consumer-provider situation arises. As one of the roles of the provider relations department is to track complaints about providers and to take corrective action where appropriate and where possible, the consumer's complaint will typically be reviewed by that department. The MCO may request those providers who evidence a pattern of consumer complaints, particularly complaints involving unethical provider practices, to terminate the MCO–provider contract. Additionally, the MCO may put a hold or a stop on all future referrals to a problematic provider pending corrective action. A problematic provider may include a provider who does not adhere to the MCO–provider contract in terms of availability and accessibility, a provider who attempts to balance bill a patient where such a practice is prohibited, a provider who has misrepresented his/her clinical expertise, a provider who does not submit appropriate treatment protocols, or a provider who is suspected, accused, or even found guilty of a more serious ethical and/or legal transgression.

The consumer must be prepared to ask the MCO about the complaint process. Frequently a grievance process is available to consumers and most MCOs do track the degree of customer satisfaction, in terms of surveys, as a routine quality assurance indicator. Commonly, consumers write letters of complaint directly to the

MCO or even directly to the payer. In some instances, consumers even call professional organizations as well as their state's insurance board. However, most complaints about providers can be handled by contacting the MCO case manager and by requesting a change in provider.

### What is medical necessity and what is denial of care? What is the difference between clinical certification and financial coverage?

Denial of care or noncertification of care generally arises when a patient's clinical presentation does not meet the particular medical necessity of care criteria espoused and followed by a specific MCO. Medical necessity criteria are practice guidelines utilized by an MCO in determining the best fit for a particular patient and a particular level or intensity of treatment. Even when there is an initial noncertification or denial of care, most MCOs afford the consumer and the provider the opportunity to appeal the decision at various levels.

As was mentioned previously, however, even where a case is found to meet the MCO's practice guidelines, clinical certification does not necessarily guarantee financial coverage of treatment by the benefit plan. Clinical certification means that a patient's presentation and level of impairment meet clinical criteria for a specific level of care. Financial coverage occurs if the patient is eligible for benefits for a specific type of care. Patients may be ineligible for benefits because they have exhausted their benefits, because they have failed to pay premiums for COBRA, or because the particular coverage has ended due to unemployment, divorce, etc. Additionally, dependent family members and spouses may not be covered under different plans.

It is important for the consumer to be aware of eligibility status as well as the procedure for ensuring coverage of a spouse and dependent(s). Further, even if a patient meets criteria for a specific level of care, the patient's benefit plan may not allow the coverage. Such may be the case in certain plans where a consumer attempts to utilize a nonparticipating provider, or where the patient has maxed out benefits for specific mental health/chemical dependency services for a given calendar or contract year. Not all benefit plans follow a calendar year and consumers having a relatively stringent health care plan must be especially aware of the time frames regarding the exhaustion of benefits, as well as the renewal of benefits.

## How do I know if I'm getting a good provider?

This concern, which is verbalized frequently by many consumers who call in for referrals, has no simple answers. For those behavioral MCOs who have carefully selected, screened, and credentialed their providers, the ability of the MCO to make a good provider referral is likely. However, in many cases, particularly in geographic areas lacking a wide selection of providers from which to choose, the chances of a good consumer–provider fit may be less than ideal. Often MCO staff, who are familiar with the performances of their various network providers, will offer suggestions to consumers as to better providers within a geographic location. Generally, consumers covered by a health plan utilizing a PPO have a greater selection of providers from which to choose and thus may be referred to providers with greater expertise and experience on average than a consumer who is limited in the choice of providers by an HMO plan, for example.

Overall, however, the more sophisticated behavioral MCOs continue to upgrade standards and performance expectations for their contracted providers to better meet the needs of the consumer. Generally, providers must meet at least minimal standards of proficiency in terms of training, experience, education, and licensing, as was noted previously. Those providers who are credentialized by MCOs must also actively participate in the case management review process and must agree to adhere to the philosophies and protocols of the particular MCO. Thus, these providers are monitored by MCO clinical staff for patient quality of care and patient outcomes. Should a consumer find a provider unsatisfactory or inappropriate for his/her treatment needs, it is probable that the MCO clinical case manager will also pick up on specific problems during the case review process.

The consumer always has recourse to change providers and to lodge complaints where necessary. The consumer can achieve a better consumer–provider fit if he/she is aware of the specific problems requiring treatment. Because many consumers do not know what to ask for, the MCO's expertise is often utilized to help the consumer in the referral process. A significant focus of MCOs is that of increasing consumer satisfaction. As such, much emphasis is placed on good consumer–provider fit to ensure treatment quality and positive clinical outcomes.

## What does *flexing* a benefit mean? How does that apply to me? Does the MCO make exceptions to my benefit package?

Flexing a benefit actually means taking an exclusion or an excluded benefit—one that is not covered by a benefit plan — and allowing it to be covered under clinically compelling or unique circumstances. As flexing a benefit is the exception rather than the rule, its occurrence varies according to the constraints of the various types of healthcare plans in which a consumer may participate. In many cases, approval from the payer must be sought by the MCO before it is able to make such an allowance.

Where it occurs, flexing of a benefit is generally done in the interest of the clinical well-being of the patient. In other cases, however, such flexing may occur due to political or administrative reasons. Cases where flexing a benefit is based on clinical judgment may be observed in the utilization of home healthcare, for example, to maintain a patient's stability and medication compliance to prevent recidivism. In other cases, coverage of a patient, such as an adolescent, in a residential program for a limited time pending placement may be allowed rather than discharging the patient to the street. Such flexing enables the provider and the patient's family to find an alternative living arrangement. In some cases, the cost of transportation to and from a hospital program may be covered in order to ensure a patient's compliance with treatment and thereby prevent rehospitalization or recidivism.

Although most consumers may never utilize flexed benefits themselves, it is important to be aware that exceptions, primarily those enabling increased patient compliance and treatment success, may be implemented. Also noteworthy is the fact that, frequently, the cost of flexing a benefit may initially be higher than simply maintaining a patient in an acute care setting. However, in the long run, flexing a benefit may well contain or decrease costs where such a provision is instrumental in reducing recidivism, particularly to a higher level of care. Positively speaking, flexing a benefit for specific patients has enabled many of them to remain outside the hospital setting for very extended periods of time. On the one hand, this practice maintains the patient in a less restrictive, more autonomous setting than a hospital and, on the other, may reduce costs generated by continued or extended hospitalizations or periods of containment.

The consumer should be reminded that a flexed benefit is clinically warranted in those cases where, without such an exception, the patient would likely deteriorate or decompensate and be rehospitalized or admitted to a more restrictive and intensive level of care. It is also warranted in those cases where placement is desirable and pending and where discharge to the street can only result in rehospitalization, for example.

### Can I use up my benefit? What happens then?

Yes, sometimes a consumer will exhaust benefits, particularly where numbers of sessions or treatment days are limited or where lifetime maximums have been reached due to prolonged illnesses. Generally, however, this is the exception, particularly given the fact that MCO staff focus on the medical necessity of treatment, often anticipating benefit limitations and offering providers alternatives where benefits are limited.

The consumer may have the option of choosing an alternative benefit plan that will allow for a greater number of treatment days or sessions or a larger lifetime maximum. In some cases, the MCO itself will make exceptions and extend treatment beyond the specified limits until the consumer's benefits are renewed for the next calendar or contract year. In other cases, MCO clinical staff will link the consumer to community resources that involve no payment or minimal payments until benefits are renewed. MCOs make it their business to monitor such a possibility and to provide alternatives.

It is important for consumers, particularly those having a limited number of sessions or treatment days within a calendar or contract year, to keep track of their particular benefit usage or utilization. The MCO staff member can frequently advise the provider on using alternatives to individual treatment, for example, to enable the consumer the best use of his or her limited coverage. In some plans, an individual session may be equivalent to two or more group sessions or one acute inpatient day may be equivalent to two or more PHP days or IOP days.

MCOs are keenly aware of the benefit allowances for particular health plans. As such, their oversight is intended to maximize the treatment a patient receives while monitoring for benefit utilization. In most cases, careful MCO clinical monitoring means reduced number of treatment sessions or days utilized, given specific medical necessity criteria. Nevertheless, the consumers are advised to be aware of any and all benefit limitations to their mental health and chemical dependency healthcare plans.

Lastly, where feasible and practical, the consumer who has maxed out benefits always has the option to self-pay for treatment. Oftentimes individual and institutional providers will work with the consumer to devise a realistic and manageable payment plan if needed.

### What if I need treatment out of state? Will I be covered?

Many health plans provide coverage should the consumer require treatment while out of state, and many behavioral care plans have locations across various states and even nationwide. Even the more restrictive benefit plans are making provisions for out-of-state coverage because such a large percentage of the population is mobile at any given time and emergencies can arise at any point. MCOs contract with particular facilities as well as with individual providers in different states for the purpose of ensuring treatment access.

Many plans will provide some degree of coverage for a consumer in the event of an emergency hospitalization; however, such plans may strongly recommend that the patient be transferred as soon as possible to an in-network provider. In contrast, however, some plans simply do not provide coverage for mental health and chemical dependency treatment in-state or out-of-state if the provider is a noncontracted or nonparticipating provider. This is often noted at intermediate levels of care such as PHP or IOP. Because there are exceptions to healthcare plans, it is recommended that the consumer question out-of-state coverage provided by the particular healthcare benefit package.

### MCO reviewers and case managers don't really know what's happening during my treatment, do they?

Yes, the objective of the majority of behavioral MCOs is to provide clinical oversight, management intervention, and education through its MCO reviewers and case managers. This means that MCO clinicians must have a working knowledge of the cases they are managing. However, the degree of intensity of clinical oversight and management may vary, depending on the particular behavioral MCO and depending on the type of case requiring clinical oversight.

MCOs will vary in the degree to which individual cases are reviewed, certified, and noncertified. In MCOs having staff shortages or having a lesser number of clinicians, this case management role may be only loosely imposed, leaving providers to telephonically review where needed. However, because the primary purpose of clinical case management is to provide medically necessary treatment and to reduce unnecessary and inappropriate utilization of services to improve quality of treatment for patients, it is very directly linked to the MCO's ability to effectively contain costs and, in many cases, realize a profit. Given these factors, many of the more sophisticated behavioral MCOs have attempted to improve the expertise of their clinical staff to more effectively manage providers, patient treatment, and, thus, overall treatment utilization.

Another factor in determining the intensity and degree of MCO clinical case management of a consumer's treatment is found in the level of intensity of the treatment being utilized or provided. Essentially, higher levels of care, such as inpatient hospitalization for treatment of psychiatric problems or detoxification and even PHP and IOP, will be more intensively case managed than routine cases such as those involving once weekly therapy. Alternatively, however, many MCOs are keenly aware of the need for intensive outpatient case management as effective oversight can mean better treatment for less time and at reduced costs. Thus, many cases in what is termed outpatient treatment and particularly those involving a high potential for recidivism to higher levels of care are also being closely case managed.

Overall, the well-trained MCO clinical case manager will attempt to grasp the consumer's current presentation in terms of problems or impairments to be addressed. The focus of MCO clinicians is on the here and now of the consumer's problems and risk level rather than on the probing and analysis of past events. Likewise, MCO providers of treatment have generally been oriented to the same brief, focused, intermittent and targeted treatment.

Although consumers often perceive the MCO clinician as simply a gatekeeper, arbitrarily authorizing and denying care, this is, with a few exceptions, rare. The use of MCO clinical staff in reviewing and managing treatment provided, serves as a safety mechanism for the consumer, primarily in that the MCO clinician will intervene where treatment is inappropriate or unnecessary. The MCO clinician serves as an advocate for the patient, fostering medically necessary treatment rather than simply medically acceptable treatment. Contracted providers are keenly aware of such oversight by the MCO and must continually strive to meet the treatment and performance standards set by both the MCO and by the consumer.

In summary, the well-trained MCO clinician will make a point of knowing a consumer's case in terms of current relevant information and will advocate for the best care in the least restrictive environment for the consumer.

### Are court-ordered services a covered benefit?

Treatment that is deemed not medically necessary is generally not clinically certified or authorized by the MCO. This applies to court-ordered treatment as well. Because treatment is court-ordered does not automatically or necessarily ensure that it meets medical necessity criteria or that it will be clinically authorized. For example, a consumer may be court-ordered to undergo five weeks of intensive outpatient chemical dependency treatment for five days per week, to comply with a court-ordered stipulation. Similarly, a court order may make a parent's visitation with offspring dependent on seeking intensive psychiatric treatment. In such cases, the MCO clinician must review a consumer's potential for risk and assess relevant impairments to determine whether a requested level of care is warranted. Hence, the MCO case management and utilization review process is the same whether treatment is court-ordered or not.

### Will my employer, family, or spouse know if I'm in treatment? How confidential is my treatment?

Except in rare exceptions, such as those involving a court- or judge-ordered subpoena for medical records, all consumers are protected by laws and ethical standards governing confidentiality of treatment. As such, no clinical records or information can be conveyed to an employer, family member, spouse, and so on unless the consumer, who is the patient, signs a release of information directing the provider(s) and/or the MCO to release treatment information. Even with a signed release of information, clinical material can only be conveyed to those parties specified by the patient. Such is the case even where parents or a legal guardian must sign for treatment for a minor child or for an adult who is deemed legally incompetent to handle his or her affairs.

As a consumer in treatment, you may be asked to sign a release of information by your provider for the provider to access treatment records or talk to a previous provider for the purposes of providing better, more targeted and focused patient care. As the consumer, you may choose to sign such a release or not. Often, in the case of minors evidencing emotional problems as well as behavioral and/or academic problems, a provider may ask the parent or legal guardian for a release of the child's school records to further clarify treatment problems and treatment goals.

To alleviate consumer and provider concerns about the loss of confidentiality, as well as to prevent potential mishandling of confidential patient information, many MCOs have gone to great lengths to prevent access to their computer systems by developing passwords. Within MCOs, patients are generally identified by initials and/or by numbers to protect confidentiality. Of course, by accepting a particular behavioral healthcare benefit package that utilizes an external MCO, the consumer has agreed to allow third-party oversight via MCO clinical staff.

Realistically, should the consumer have concerns about confidentiality, the consumer is advised to question the MCO and/or the provider of the treatment regarding the process utilized in safeguarding treatment information.

### I don't know what kind of treatment I need. Who can help me? What if I need medication?

Frequently, an MCO will receive a call from a consumer who feels the need for treatment but who does not know what the treatment options are. This is a very common occurrence. Whereas in the case of a crisis call, an MCO clinician would ensure the patient's transport and admission to a hospital or some other type of immediate crisis intervention, general or typical consumer calls are less risky and generally more routine in nature. However, MCO staff review consumer calls for risk status and treatment need to provide the best consumer–provider fit. Because clinical staff review all treatment cases against medical necessity criteria, the consumer of treatment is in a very good position to access provider information. The MCO clinician can advise the consumer on whether family, couples, group, or individual treatment, or some combination of these, is needed to meet the consumer's needs. Further, as risk assessment is an integral part of clinical case review, an assessment of a consumer's need for medication is generally performed throughout the course of treatment, from the initial review through the concurrent reviews and even on termination of therapy. Oftentimes, a consumer of treatment may continue to see a psychiatrist for psychotropic medication management long after a specific therapy episode is completed.

Although the consumer is directed by the MCO staff towards the best fit in terms of provider and types or levels of treatment, the consumer can always disagree with the treatment decision or referral or request a change in provider and / or a change in the type, the frequency, or the intensity of treatment.

### What if I want to stay with the therapist I've been with in the past and the therapist is a noncontracted provider or a nonparticipating provider?

Although most behavioral healthcare plans attempt to link consumers with their own contracted providers, often a consumer will request a transition to a provider with whom the consumer has had a prior relationship, and who also happens to be a nonparticipating provider. This request is frequently noted in cases where a consumer is being transitioned from a higher level of care to a less intensive level of care, such as outpatient treatment.

Generally, even the most stringent healthcare plans will make exceptions regarding coverage at the enhanced or standard benefit rate. This is particularly true in cases where linkage to the nonparticipating provider is considered in the best clinical interest of the patient in terms of treatment compliance and preventing recidivism. Sometimes, nonparticipating providers are utilized as experts in certain areas such as in medication management or in the treatment of affective disorders. It is not uncommon for an MCO to refer a more clinically complex or difficult case to such a nonparticipating expert and to pick up the entire fee for services rendered in order to ensure optimal patient care. Providing necessary treatment expertise at the front end may well decrease recidivism and thus long-range costs.

However, many HMO behavioral healthcare benefits rarely allow for such exceptions, and even in less restrictive plans, treatment with a noncontracted provider is generally not encouraged and many result in greater out-of-pocket expenses for the consumer.

In those cases where exceptions are made for sound clinical reasons, the MCO will attempt to negotiate a rate with a provider that is more compatible with the rates paid to their already contracted providers. Naturally, this system has both pros and cons. On one hand, the consumer may not always be able to access the provider requested. Alternatively, the patient tends to receive treatment that is more highly scrutinized for clinical necessity and appropriateness because the MCO manages its contracted or participating providers.

Overall, MCOs attempt to inform consumers regarding the status of a provider. The consumer may choose to see a nonparticipating provider regardless of the MCO's recommendation and, thus, the consumer may pay a larger percentage of the provider fee.

### What happens in case of an emergency? How can I get help?

Most, if not all, MCOs have an emergency number, usually an 800 number, that can be accessed 24 hours a day. Generally, MCO clinicians handle emergencies or crises during regular working hours. Often, however, consumers may require emergency treatment after hours. MCO clinicians working after regular workday hours will handle such cases in much the same way that crises are handled during regular work hours. This includes emergencies occurring on the weekends and during holidays. With few exceptions, the expectations regarding precertification even after hours are consistent with those during regular working hours.

### Do I have any say in my own treatment? What are my rights? Can I refuse treatment?

The consumer's active participation in treatment is an integral component to the treatment episode. The consumer of treatment determines treatment problems and goals together with the provider and, hence, indirectly with the MCO case manager. This goal setting serves to establish an appropriate endpoint for treatment. However, at any point, the consumer may decline treatment or simply terminate treatment. With the exception of such events as a commitment hearing in mental health court, where treatment is mandated by the judge, subscribers often end treatment for a variety of reasons. Even hospitalized consumers of treatment leave AMA (against medical advice) or ASA (against staff advice).

Termination of treatment by a consumer tends to become problematic when a pattern of shopping for a provider or a type of treatment comes to the attention of the MCO. This scenario is often found where the consumer is ambivalent about treatment, is being forced into treatment, or where the very nature of the psychiatric problem significantly impacts the consumer's ability to exercise judgment, to make a commitment to treatment, and to comply with treatment. In cases where this pattern of shopping arises, MCO clinical staff will generally attempt to contact both the consumer and the provider of care such that an appropriate plan of action can be implemented should the consumer continue to follow this pattern.

The consumer has numerous rights, that are protected by law, by professional ethical standards and by consumer or patient advocacy or watchdog groups, as they are often called. Essentially, these rights include, among others, the right to confidentiality, the right to freedom from abuse of any sort, and the right to question treatment and to refuse treatment. For a more comprehensive listing of patient rights, the consumer may request a copy from the MCO and from the provider. With rare exceptions, denial or disregard of these rights may result in provider sanctioning, MCO staff warnings and/or dismissal, and in some cases, legal ramifications, including the loss of licensure.

### What are all these letters I'm getting? What do they really mean?

Most MCOs have standard form letters for a variety of protocols and procedures ranging from outpatient referrals to payment notifications, to noncertification of clinical treatment. Although the wording of specific letters varies across behavioral MCOs, they will generally address similar issues. Frequently, this correspondence can be highly confusing to the consumer. MCO staff, particularly the clinician assigned to manage the treatment, is often the consumer's best resource in answering questions about clinical issues such as non-certification, nonprecertification, referrals, and so on.

Other letters may be generated from the provider relations department, the customer service department, administration, the intake department, the medical carrier, if it exists, and the payer. The consumer is advised to note the name as well as the department or organization from which the letter was generated. Consumers are also advised to check correspondence for any errors in treatment information and in the payment of claims. When in doubt, contact the MCO for clarification or correction. It is common practice for MCOs to keep all parties informed regarding certification status, payment status, exhaustion of benefit status, and so forth. Do not be surprised at receiving multiple correspondence from your MCO.

### My provider can't see me anymore because he is not getting paid or he has no more treatment sessions left. What is my responsibility in such a case?

This, unfortunately, is a very common complaint among consumers and providers and may be mishandled by either the provider, the MCO staff, or both. Realistically, the situation does occur where, for one reason or another, a provider has not received payment from the MCO, and the consumer of treatment is caught in the middle. The consumer is advised to refer the provider back to the MCO for payment resolution.

Often consumers will be informed by providers that treatment cannot continue due to the lack of any more clinically authorized sessions for treatment. This is particularly noteworthy in outpatient treatment. The consumer should be aware that most health care contracts require the provider of services and/or the consumer to precertify for all patient treatment. Further, most situations such as these can usually be readily remedied by calling the MCO case manager. In some cases, however, the provider will not receive further clinical certification for patient treatment because the consumer has truly exhausted the behavioral healthcare benefits for the calendar or contract year.

In other cases a simpler explanation exists. Often the provider will fail to keep track of outpatient sessions and thus continue treatment beyond the certified date. Additionally, the provider may have neglected to send in necessary paperwork to the MCO justifying continued certification. Also, the provider may have attempted to pursue further certification but was unable to reach the appropriate MCO staff. These cases are easily corrected by calling the MCO. The consumer will find that, given such explanations, certification will be rendered if medically necessary, and, in most cases, the consumer will not be penalized.

### What is meant by custodial care? Is it a covered benefit? If not, who can help me financially?

Generally, in most healthcare plans, placement in what is called a residential program is often not a covered benefit. Of course, there are exceptions. MCOs notify consumers where specific types or levels of care are excluded from the benefit package. Custodial care means basically that a person is placed in a setting where he or she can receive coverage for medically necessary treatment, but where room and board are generally excluded. Generally the patient, the patient's family, or the subscriber must pay for room and board. MCO clinical staff may direct the consumer to a school district and to some community agencies that can be accessed to assist in financial coverage for some portion of the uncovered services. In the case of adolescents, for example, some school districts will cover educational expenses plus a portion of the room and board. Often, MCOs suggest that the consumer contact the provider of care in an effort to negotiate manageable payment terms. Although some providers are unable to negotiate, often providers do have flexibility. When in doubt, the consumer is advised to call the MCO regarding whether or not residential treatment or placement is a covered benefit.

### Are special services available to me if I am hearing impaired or speak a different language?

Yes, most MCOs do provide specialized services. MCOs deal with consumers across a variety of different cultures, and most MCOs render behavioral care services to consumers with special needs. However, it is up to the consumer to ask about the availability of such services. Those MCOs having a wide range of providers will have providers who speak different languages as well as providers who handle chemical dependency and mental health treatment for consumers with special needs. Further, MCOs will frequently contract out for specialized services, if they are unable to utilize their own providers.

### Do I really need to stay in this program for three weeks? How do I know if I need all these services?

The role of the MCO is to determine the medical necessity of care. As such, the MCO clinician is an advocate for the best care that can be provided for a patient. The role of the clinical case manager is to readily determine whether or not a patient requires the services being rendered. In many cases, services are appropriate; however, often services may be too extensive in terms of frequency, intensity, or duration. It is the role of the case manager to intervene with the provider if such is the case. If you, as the consumer, have a question about the efficacy or the appropriateness of the treatment you are receiving, you need to contact the MCO to review your concerns.

It should be noted that many providers may not be aware of alternative treatment strategies and may thus continue or perpetuate the concept that treatment must occur over a certain period of time. It is at this point that the MCO case manager can intervene to offer the provider options or different ways of conducting treatment such that the consumer of care is assured the least restrictive type of treatment, that is brief, focused, and targeted.

### What community resources are available and how can I find out about them?

Again, the consumer's best resource for accessing community services is generally through the clinical case manager assigned to the case and the provider. Since the least restrictive treatment setting is integral to managed care philosophy, community support groups are strongly encouraged by MCO clinicians. These may include such groups as Overeaters Anonymous, Parents Without Partners, bereavement groups, and so forth.

### I often feel that I don't know what practice guidelines the MCO is utilizing to make decisions. Can I get a copy of the MCO's medical necessity guidelines?

More and more MCOs are realizing the importance of education for their own staff as well as for providers and consumers of treatment regarding the clinical or medical necessity criteria they utilize to make decisions about clinical certification and clinical noncertification. As communication has increased among consumers, providers, and MCO staff and as the importance of positive provider–MCO relations has become more significant, access to specific materials such as medical necessity guidelines or practice guidelines has become easier. For a fee, the provider as well as the consumer generally can purchase a copy of the particular MCO's guidelines. Often, the consumer or provider can get information about medical necessity criteria by simply calling the MCO clinical case manager. Consumers and providers are encouraged to ask questions. Only through open communication among all parties, that is consumers of care, providers of care, and MCOs who manage care, will there be positive outcomes in terms of optimal patient care, that is clinically effective as well as cost-effective.

## REFERENCE

Baldor, Robert A. 1996. *Managed Care Made Simple*. Cambridge, MA: Blackwell Science, Inc.

# 9

# LONG RANGE SURVIVAL IN BEHAVIORAL MANAGED CARE: WORKING THE SYSTEM

## FUTURE TRENDS AND MONEY-MAKING CONCEPTS

Ideally the present can tell much about the future of behavioral managed care and prepare MCOs, providers, and patients for changes and trends. This section focuses on some specific trends that will clinically, administratively, and financially affect the treatment of mental health and chemical dependency. Although not exhaustive, they may help providers in particular to plan creatively.

### Case-Rate Contracts and Macromanagement

Currently, contracting by MCOs with providers, specifically large organizations such as hospitals and practice groups, is increasing. Case-rate contracts can take various forms, but essentially they give a larger share of the financial risk to providers. Basically, multispecialty or multilevel care providers agree to a rate mutually established with the MCO for each patient for different levels of care or for a level of care such as inpatient treatment. Depending on the specific contract, the provider receives a certain preset amount of money for any patient who enters a particular treatment level. This case rate is intended to cover the entire gamut of that patient's treatment episode within specified time frames. For example, Hospital A agrees to a rate of $3,000 to cover the cost of patient B's treatment. This treatment may range from one day of inpatient treatment to multiple days or weeks of treatment at the various levels of care, including IP, PHP, and so on. Although this is a simplified example, specific financial incentives are apparent. Generally,

1. The participating provider assumes greater financial risk for a patient's care and must attempt to remain below the specified case rate per patient if it is to profit financially.

2. Several levels of patient care may be considered as one treatment episode and must be managed by the provider under the preset case rate, depending on the contract.

3. Depending on the contract negotiated, specific time periods are designated such that patient recidivism is covered by the provider after which point the MCO may make financial adjustments. The incentives for the provider to ensure workable aftercare and to discharge patients where clinically stable from more costly levels of care, such as inpatient treatment, are significant.

4. The incentive to reduce the length of time the patient spends in a PHP, for example, is also significant, if the provider is to profit. For example, even if a patient is discharged from inpatient within two days, the profit to the provider will be minimal, at best, if the patient remains in a PHP for many weeks. The potential incentive to modify PHPs as they exist today also appears noteworthy. Although many providers currently request a specified number of days or weeks of treatment for a specified amount of time, provider practices will undoubtedly change. Case-rate contracts will alter the goals, structure, and outcomes of these intermediate levels of care. Now is the time for industrious providers to develop workable alternatives to these traditional programs.

5. Although the incentive to admit a patient for at least one day of treatment to access the case rate is extremely high, the motivation to discharge into a less expensive but more effective alternate care site is also very significant. The question, however, is where are such levels of care that will adequately fit this bill? Developing and implementing new approaches to alternate care sites continues to challenge providers as well as MCOs.

6. Macromanagement by MCOs of large providers has been in place for some time; however, the increasingly shared responsibility of risk by providers, in conjunction with MCOs, will necessarily increase the frequency of macromanagement. Such providers will be actively involved in their own management and review of treatment

with MCOs serving in a greater educational resource role than before. Necessarily, providers who have been accustomed to MCO micromanagement of individual cases will need to formulate internal controls for treatment services and cost containment.

## Crisis Intervention Teams

With providers becoming more financially and clinically invested and responsible for their own treatment services and with MCOs taking more of an educational or consultant role, the need for easily accessible and immediate crisis intervention is significantly increasing. Though mobile crisis teams have always been utilized, their significance as a primary intervention prior to a patient's admission to a level of care, particularly inpatient treatment, is increasing.

Currently, both MCOs and contracted providers utilize such crisis teams to assess risk, to diffuse crisis situations, where possible, and to deflect admissions to higher levels of care that might have been the only patient option in the past. With the increase in risk-sharing by providers, the focus of these crisis teams is a hands-on approach to initiating necessary crisis linkage and initiating the treatment plan at the time and site of intervention. This means that crisis team members need immediate or near-immediate access to providers willing and able to treat patients quickly and effectively. While most aftercare discharge planning is currently performed during the course of a patient's treatment in a specific level of care, the future use of crisis teams requires immediate access and linkage to providers, as well as to ancillary services such as home health, transportation, medication consults, and community support groups. It also requires access to available and brief alternative living arrangements within the community.

Currently, many of the larger, multifaceted providers perform these functions for MCOs who provide them with financial incentives. However, even the best-intentioned providers are limited by limitations in community resources. For example, access to programs, particularly on weekends, is quite limited, as is the availability of many ancillary services.

Noteworthy is the fact that these triage services will often be performed in less controlled environments, such as in emergency rooms of large hospitals where crisis teams and emergency room staff are unfamiliar with each other and come from diverse backgrounds. In such circumstances, the need for highly trained and experienced crisis workers who are clinically sophisticated in rapid risk assessment as well as in treatment linkage is paramount to the success of patient stabilization and deflection to less restrictive environments.

MCOs and providers alike are motivated to provide the best patient care with very limited treatment resources, limited time, and limited financial support. Doing so requires creative and innovative problem solving. It is likely that the clinical and financial incentives motivating providers and MCOs to adapt to the current trends will result in programs and services that are quite different in goals, structures, and patient treatment acuity from programs currently in place. Individual clinicians, as well as larger providers, are advised to take a careful look at what they can offer, given these changes. It is probable that more institutional providers will either specialize in specific clinical areas, such as in the 24-hour access to the biopsychosocial treatment of depression, or they will develop a one-stop shopping approach. This approach will provide immediate access to clinical treatment, medication evaluation, home healthcare, emergency living arrangements, and so on. Now is the time to review what you, as the provider, can bring to the table to ensure your clinical and economic viability as behavioral managed care undergoes another evolution.

## Home Health Care Agencies/Visiting Nurse Associations (VNA)

The increased awareness of the need to provide alternative, less restrictive treatment options and to offer immediate access to treatment has propelled a proliferation of various home healthcare groups and agencies.

It is my professional opinion, having recommended and utilized these services for patients in a variety of situations, that home health is a key component of current and future behavioral managed care. As such, these groups will continue to require increasingly sophisticated methods for meeting the challenges of patient needs. Consider the following points as evidence of the significance of home healthcare services.

1. Behavioral managed care provides a financial incentive to providers to avoid hospitalizations and to decrease time spent in acute treatment when an individual is hospitalized. Further, managed care has resulted in a decrease in the time spent even in intermediate levels of care such as PHP and IOP. However, providers servicing these care levels frequently have limited to no access to alternative options for their patients. Even if they discharge patients quickly on stabilization, recidivism is likely with corresponding financial losses. This dilemma is commonplace and providers justifiably question the clinical and financial soundness of discharging a patient from a level of care, without effective supports, only to have the patient return to that level of care or to an even higher level of care.

The answer, in part, is found in home health services. Visiting nurse associations and other such groups regularly employ licensed social workers, RNs, LPNs, and aids to ensure medication compliance, support in the home, access to other providers, as well as mental status or risk monitoring, to name a few. Further, they can provide 24-hour services and will often tailor these services to fit a patient's needs. Although many hospitals have access to their own home healthcare agencies, providers are often unaware of the variety of functions that these groups can perform. With the aggressive management of providers and patient care by behavioral MCOs, however, VNA and other healthcare groups are increasingly promoted as viable options to the potential revolving-door syndrome.

2. One of the major treatment, as well as financial, challenges facing providers and MCOs is the prevention of recidivism in the chronic patient population. Often such patients are medication-noncompliant and socially isolated, increasing their potential for rehospitalization. Home healthcare can provide a viable alternative to inpatient treatment, as well as aid in the prevention of recidivism. By going into the patient's home environment to provide treatment, medication, transportation to treatment in the community and other services, home health groups can often successfully intervene, thus avoiding a rehospitalization. Naturally, some patients will continue to require hospitalization regardless of the interventions utilized.

3. Down time and evening and holiday hours are often periods of increased patient utilization of services. In many cases, 24-hour accessibility to support and crisis intervention by home healthcare

staff can prevent a full-blown treatment episode. This is particularly noted with older individuals and adolescents.

4. Many patients lack the financial resources to cover the expense of medication renewal and transportation to therapists. They are often unaware of how to access disability or even how to locate support from community self-help groups. Others may require assistance in performing basic functions in the home due to the severity of their illnesses or may have significant medical problems that complicate their psychiatric illnesses. Home healthcare can effectively handle many of these problems.

5. Frequently, MCOs and providers do not know whether a patient is following up with aftercare treatment and if not, why not. Effective aftercare linkage and follow-through is frequently out of the control of most providers. However, noncompliance with treatment linkage is a significant contributing factor to recidivism. Home health, through its outreach, can make a dent in this problem. Even in cases where hospitalization is unavoidable, the presence of home healthcare can assure the provider of decreased patient risk on discharge and possibly a briefer inpatient stay. Very significantly, home health services provide the missing link between the provider, the patient, and the MCO. Home health encourages communication with aftercare providers and MCOs regarding the status of particular patients, thus making timely intervention more likely to occur. By becoming familiar with the patient in his or her home environment, healthcare workers can often notify the provider about potential treatment problems and probable reasons for noncompliance. Oftentimes a patient will not divulge the fact that medication side effects, for example, are the cause of his or her not taking medications. However, a home healthcare staff is more likely to determine this through observation of and discussion with the patient. Some patients feel intimidated by licensed providers and are more apt to disclose information to home healthcare aides with whom they feel more at ease. Home healthcare staff also effectively convey information to providers about what is working and what is not working with a particular patient, thus enabling the provider to change treatment accordingly.

The advantages of utilizing home healthcare are significant; however, home healthcare is also undergoing changes to meet the demands of new trends in the delivery of mental health and substance abuse treatment. Specifically, home health is reexamining the following critical aspects of its own delivery systems.

- 24-hour accessibility for crisis situations.
- Provision of specialty services.
- Expertise of staff: use of multidisciplinary teams to handle all aspects of treatment.
- Geographic access, particularly to more isolated, remote locations where services are badly needed.
- System of communication with providers and MCOs regarding patient treatment.
- Ability to access community support in terms of financial, clinical, transportation, housing, and other services.
- System of protocols and procedures for handling the variety of treatment problems.
- Implementation of effective networking with other treatment systems in the community to ensure bridges to any gaps in service options.
- Increased visibility and promotion of home health services to community groups and providers through the media and presentations, and so on.
- Compliance with accrediting bodies regarding paperwork, procedures, licensing, and so forth.
- Development of specific outcome studies of treatment success and failure.
- Development of cost-effective services, that will promote high patient, provider, and MCO usage.

These are a few of the factors being redefined by home health-care currently. Recognition of the potentially integral role of home health is the first step in establishing a sophisticated and treatment-effective system. This type of service will continue to change and evolve as the market sets new expectations for MCOs, providers, and consumers.

## Providers and Provider Groups

As has been noted previously, recent trends in managed care suggest that providers will need to increase their clinical sophistication to meet current market demands and also to remain financially viable. The move towards single specialty and one-stop shopping will continue, particularly if providers are to assume greater shared clinical and financial risk for patients. Providers need to package their products using business savvy and successful marketing strategies. The competition among providers is tough and requires a knowledge of market demands. Many successful managed care providers have taken the necessary steps already to ensure decreased recidivism as well as treatment that is targeted and focused. As MCOs themselves become more clinically sophisticated, the demand for a thorough understanding of the language and symbols of managed care will increase. Providers will be required to provide data to support their treatment strategies and will be required to make adjustments where strategies are deemed unsuccessful. Like any product, selling mental health and chemical dependency treatment to the market (patients, subscribers, other providers, MCOs, etc.) means providing a service that is unique, outcome-effective, enduring, and cost-efficient.

Currently, behavioral managed care trends indicate the need for: (1) crisis intervention and stabilization, (2) quick and easy access to workable alternatives to traditional levels of care, and (3) philosophical and programmatic changes in existing treatment programs. As a provider, you might consider the following questions in determining your marketability.

1. How accessible are your services?
2. Can you provide crisis intervention and stabilization?
3. How well do you know community resources and can you access them readily?
4. Do you have a particular specialty that is significantly different from that offered by other providers in terms of outcome, cost, or accessibility?
5. How visible are you to consumers, other providers, MCOs, and so on?
6. Have you considered publicizing your services to an MCO, to another provider, or to a consumer group?
7. Can you provide a particular resource that is scarce or difficult to access?
8. Are you sufficiently familiar with managed care to know the language and to deliver the necessary paperwork?

9. What geographic locations can you cover and what aspects of your staff are unique?
10. Why are your services needed in the managed care market?
11. Can you provide services geared to difficult cases such as chronic, high recidivist patients?
12. What gap in the current service delivery system can you fill and how?
13. Can you develop alternate programs that will better meet the current treatment demands? How?
14. What proof of success do you have? How will you make your services more successful?
15. What market demands do you intend to meet in the future?

In summary, these are a few of the trends occurring in behavioral managed care that require attention. The demands of the consumer, the availability of resources, and the amount of money allotted to treatment will all affect the existing and future quality and structure of the service delivery system for mental health and chemical dependency. The contributions of patients, consumers, providers, and MCOs in shaping the goals, the quality, and the outcomes of this system will continue to provide the foundation on which behavioral managed care currently exists and develops its future course. Good luck to all of us!

# BIBLIOGRAPHY

American Psychiatric Association. 1995. *Diagnostic and Statistical Manual of Mental Disorders*, 4th edition (DSM IV). Washington, DC: American Psychiatric Press.

Austad, Carol S., and William H. Berman, eds. 1991. *Psychotherapy in Managed Health Care: The Optimum Use of Time and Money*. Washington, DC: American Psychological Association.

Baldor, Robert A. 1996. *Managed Care Made Simple*. Cambridge, MA: Blackwell Science, Inc.

Bennett, Michael J., M.D. 1996. "Is Psychotherapy Ever Medically Necessary?" *Psychiatric Services* 47, no. 9 (September): 996–970.

Cafferky, Michael E. 1995. *Managed Care and You: The Consumer's Guide to Managing Your Health Care*. New York: McGraw-Hill.

Feldman, Judith L., and Richard Fitzpatrick, eds. 1992. *Managed Mental Health Care: Administrative and Clinical Issues*. Washington, DC: American Psychiatric Press, Inc.

Freeman, Michael A., and Tom Trabin. 1994. "Managed Behavioral Health Care: History, Models, Key Issues, and Future Course." Rockville, Maryland: Paper prepared for the U.S. Center for Mental Health Services, Department of Health and Human Services, October.

HFCA. 1994. "Managed Care Growth Continues in Private, Public Sectors." *Behavioral Healthcare Tomorrow* 4, no. 3 (May/June): 8.

Hoyt, Michael F. 1995. *Brief Therapy and Managed Care*. San Francisco, CA: Jossey-Bass Publishers.

Hymowitz, Carol, and Ellen Joan Pollack. 1995. "Psychobattle." In the New Economics of Mental Health Series. *The Wall Street Journal* (Midwest Edition), July 13.

Kelley, Timothy. 1994. "10 Charges Leveled against Managed Mental Health Care." *Managed Care: A Guide for Physicians* 3, no. 10 (October): 22–26.

Klebanoff, Nina A. and Catherine Boubin Casler. 1996. "The Psychosocial Clinical Nurse Specialist: An Untapped Resource for Home Care." *Home Healathcare Nurse* 4, no. 6: 36–40.

Lowman, Rodney L., and Robert J. Resnick, eds. 1994. *The Mental Health Professional's Guide to Managed Care*. Washington, DC: American Psychological Association.

MacKenzie, K. Roy, M.D., editor. 1995. *Effective Use of Group Therapy in Managed Care*. Washington, DC: American Psychiatric Press.

Marulle, John A. 1994. "Medical Education Takes on a Managed Care Flavor." *Managed Care: A Guide for Physicians* 3, no. 10 (October): 28–33.

Mechanic, D., and L. H. Aiken. 1989. "Capitation in Mental Health: Potentials and Cautions." *New Directions in Mental Health Services* 43: 5–18.

Miller, Ivan J. Ph.D. 1994. *What Manged Care Is Doing to Outpatient Mental Health.* Boulder, CO: Boulder Psychotherapists' Press, Inc.

Oss, Monica E., and Stair Trev, eds. 1996. *Managed Behavioral Health Care in the United States, 1996–1997.* Gettysburg, PA: OPEN Minds Publication, Behaviorial Health Industry News, Inc.

Phillips, E. Lakin. 1988. *Patient Compliance: New Light on Health Delivery Systems in Medicine and Psychotherapy.* Toronto, Canada: Hans Huber Publishers.

Roberts, Bruce, M.D. 1980. "A Computerized Diagnostic Evaluation of a Psychiatric Problem." *American Journal of Psychiatry* 137, no. 1 (January).

Roberts, Bruce, M.D. 1984. "Computers in the Psychiatric Evaluation Process." *Update: Computers in Medicine* II, no. 1 (January/February).

Roberts, Bruce, M.D. 1996. "A Focused, Efficient Overview of Psychiatric Managed Care." Unpublished paper.

Roberts, Bruce, M.D. 1996. "Quality as the Driving Force in Cost-Effective Psychiatric Managed Care." *Journal for Healthcare Quality* 18, no. 1 (January/February): 4–8.

Sharfstein, S.S. 1992. "Managed Mental Health Care." In *Review of Psychiatry* 11, A. Tasman and A. B. Riba, eds., 570–84. Washington, DC: American Psychiatric Press.

Shueman, Sharon A., Warwick G. Troy, and Samuel L. Mayhugh, eds. 1994. *Managed Behavioral Health Care: An Industry Perspective.* Springfield, IL: Charles C. Thomas Publishing.

Theis, Gerald A. 1994. "Quality Outcome Measurements Relevant to Behavioral Health Services." *AAPPO Journal* (January/February): 10–13.

Tuttle, Gayle and Associates, eds. 1996. "Managed Care Special Report." *Practical Strategies* 2, no. 8 (August): 1–9.

Winegar, Norman. 1992. *The Clinician's Guide to Managed Mental Health Care.* New York: The Haworth Press, Inc.

Winegar, Norman, and J. L. Bistline. 1994. *Marketing Mental Health Services in a Managed Care Environment.* New York: The Haworth Press, Inc.

Wynn, Paul. 1995. "The Public's View on Managed Care: A Fuzzy One." *Managed Care: A Guide for Physicians* 4, no. 12 (December): 9.

# INDEX

## J–L

## M